Paul S. Underwood

The Manager
and Economic Reform
in Hungary

Geza Peter Lauter

The Praeger Special Studies program—utilizing the most modern and efficient book production techniques and a selective worldwide distribution network—makes available to the academic, government, and business communities significant, timely research in U.S. and international economic, social, and political development.

The Manager and Economic Reform in Hungary

PRAEGER SPECIAL STUDIES IN INTERNATIONAL ECONOMICS AND DEVELOPMENT

Praeger Publishers   New York   Washington   London

PRAEGER PUBLISHERS
111 Fourth Avenue, New York, N.Y. 10003, U.S.A.
5, Cromwell Place, London S.W.7, England

Published in the United States of America in 1972
by Praeger Publishers, Inc.

© 1972 by Praeger Publishers, Inc.

Library of Congress Catalog Card Number: 76-161910

Printed in the United States of America

To Eva-Maria

In the global economic competition marked by the United States as the most developed and most powerful representative of the capitalist countries and by the Soviet Union as the oldest and most influential representative of the socialist world, Hungary is a small, and perhaps inconsequential, competitor. With a population of a little over 10 million people and an essentially semideveloped economy, Hungary rarely captures the imagination of the world, as do, for better or for worse, the United States and the Soviet Union, on occasion.

On January 1, 1968, however, through the introduction of a set of economic reforms, this small but enterprising nation made global news. Since that time, managers and economic scholars of both the capitalist and the socialist world have been following Hungarian economic developments with interest. They are doing so because, in a larger context, Hungary's New Economic Mechanism (NEM) represents more than just the attempts of a semideveloped nation to improve its industrialization process and to raise its standard of living. The reform also represents an attempt to combine the most useful features of the socialist economic system with the most useful and politically acceptable features of capitalism in order to create a flexible and humane socialist strategy of industrialization. The events in the Eastern European socialist countries since the 1950's have shown that the formulation of such a strategy is long overdue.

It is the objective of this book to present a discussion of the major features of NEM, to point out its current industrial management problems, and to assess its probable future course. The book's focus is on the nature and implications of industrial-management problems, because the long-run success of the reform depends chiefly on the performance of the

managers, who are charged with the day-to-day implementation and management of the reform at the enterprise level. Thus, purely political, economic, and
social issues are discussed only to the extent that
they help in understanding managerial behavior and
problems.

The term "managers" is applied throughout the
book to refer to (as they are known in the Eastern
European socialist countries and in the literature)
the industrial-enterprise director, his immediate
deputies, and major departmental heads. Since Hungarian industrial enterprises tend to be highly centralized, this group of managers represents the locus
of decision-making authority throughout Hungarian
industry. The terms "reformers" and "central authorities" are used interchangeably and refer to the
heads of government agencies charged with the over-
all direction of the country's economic life and
with the supervision of industrial enterprises.

The discussion of as vast a subject as the fundamental reorganization of an economic and managerial
system is bound to be limited in several respects.
To maintain the managerial orientation of the book,
the material had to be organized in a special way.
To keep the topic manageable, it was necessary to
treat some issues more lightly than others. Finally,
to explore the implications of complex and highly
interrelated issues, errors of perception and interpretation were probably unavoidable.

This work is based on the evaluation of chiefly
Hungarian secondary sources, such as government publications, academic studies, periodicals, magazines,
and newspapers. The information thus obtained was
supplemented, during visits to Hungary, by discussions with managers, workers, academicians, and consumers. The book is the result of a study sponsored
by the Committee on Research of The George Washington University. In addition to this committee, I am
indebted to Angela Wray for her invaluable editorial
assistance.

                                        Geza Peter Lauter

Washington, D.C.
October, 1971

CONTENTS

x

LIST OF TABLES

LIST OF FIGURES

TRANSLATION OF FREQUENTLY CITED
HUNGARIAN PERIODICALS

Figyelö   Observer

Gazdaság   Economics

Marketing-Piackutatás   Marketing-Market Research

Népszabadság   People's Freedom

The Manager
and Economic Reform
in Hungary

At the end of World War II, Hungary, like most of Europe, was in ruins. Several years of hard work and sacrifice on the part of the entire population were necessary to rebuild the country to a point where normal life was again possible. The rebuilding efforts involved, among other steps, the restarting of industrial and agricultural production, the repair of the transportation system, and the introduction of a new currency into the inflation-ridden economy.

The years of rebuilding were marked by severe struggles among the newly formed political parties. These clashes resulted in a change from a coalition government to a single-party rule, and, by 1949, the Hungarian economy was reorganized along the lines of the centrally planned Soviet economic system.

THE MANAGER AND THE ECONOMY, 1949-56

The first step in reorganizing the economy along the lines of the Soviet model was the large-scale nationalization effort started shortly after the end of World War II. By March, 1948, almost all industrial enterprises employing more than 100 workers had been expropriated. Simultaneously with the nationalization efforts, the First Three-Year Plan was introduced in 1947. The plan was designed to attain prewar

industrial and agricultural output levels, to raise
the standard of living, and to start building the
heavy industrial base believed necessary for the
creation of a socialist society.

To this end, the specific plan objectives included annual industrial and agricultural production
quotas, detailed investment-outlay requirements, and
expected labor-productivity increases. Initially,
these specific objectives were not forced upon the
various industries in an arbitrary manner; in most
cases, industry representatives and government officials worked out the plans together. Modifications
were easily possible, and, in general, a spirit of
cooperation prevailed.

The system of cooperation, however, was replaced
in 1949, when over-all development and administration
of the plan became the sole responsibility of the
newly formed People's Economic Council and the National Planning Office. These two top organizations
were supported by several directorates that represented many different industries and that were later
charged with the day-to-day management of the enterprises under their authority.

Accomplishment of the plan objectives called for
an extremely high rate of capital accumulation. Since
foreign capital aid was excluded, new capital had to
be generated from domestic sources. This necessitated
a policy of austerity, and its burden had to be carried by the entire population. Compulsory saving
became imperative and was achieved chiefly through
taxation. Investment-fund allocations by the central
authorities were made on the basis of predetermined
priorities, which were mainly of a political nature.
In general, the allocations favored heavy industry
over all other branches of the economy.

Prices were controlled by the Office of Price
Control to ensure the effectiveness of planning on
an economy-wide basis. The aim was not to bring
about an equilibrium of supply and demand but chiefly
to prevent any price movements that could affect cost
calculations and wage policies negatively. (Wages,

which were set through collective-bargaining agreements, had to be approved by the central authorities.)

     During the plan period, which ended in 1949, most
of the foreign-trade sector was nationalized, and
trade in selected products became a government monopoly. The newly formed Hungarian Foreign Trade Directorate was charged with the administration of trade
relations. Soon afterward, however, the directorate
was abolished and replaced by the Ministry of Foreign
Trade.

     In terms of its objectives, the First Three-Year
Plan was a modest success.[1] Industrial and agricultural production was restored to prewar levels, and
the resulting standard of living provided most Hungarian citizens with a frugal, but acceptable, way
of life. Most of all, the government completed the
nationalization of all sectors of the economy and,
through forced capital accumulation, established the
necessary base for the large-scale industrialization
efforts of the following years.

First Five-Year Plan, 1950-54

     At the start of the First Five-Year Plan, on
January 1, 1950, the Hungarian Working People's Party
was in control of the country and the political
transformation of Hungary had been completed. The
plan, accordingly, was developed entirely along the
lines of the doctrinaire Soviet planning model. Its
general objective was to "build the foundations of
socialism" and, in the process of so doing, transform
Hungary not only from an agrarian-industrial country
into an industrial-agrarian one but also into an
"iron and steel country" (a phrase coined by Ernö
Gerö, the very able and hard-driving minister who
was in charge of the economy).

     The specific objectives of the plan were set
very high.[2] By 1954, for example, national income
was to be increased 63 per cent over the 1949 level;
total industrial output, 86 per cent; heavy industrial production, 104 per cent; and agricultural
output, 42 per cent. By the end of the planning

period, the standard of living was to be 35 per cent
higher than in the base year. The plan also specified
that 25 per cent of national income was to be devoted
to new investments and that 42 per cent of this amount
had to be invested in the industrial sector of the
economy. Heavy industry was to receive 86 per cent
of this amount. In contrast, only 16 per cent of
total investment funds were earmarked for agricultural
development.

Thus, the groundwork for unbalanced economic
growth was established. At the Second Congress of
the Hungarian Working People's Party in 1951, the
situation was worsened when the original targets
were drastically revised. According to the new
targets, 30 per cent of national income was to be
reinvested. The share of industrial investments was
to be raised from 42 per cent to 47 per cent and that
of agricultural investments was to be reduced from
16 per cent to 15 per cent. Industrial output was
expected to increase an almost unbelievable 210 per
cent over the 1949 level, instead of the initially
projected 86 per cent. To this increase, heavy industry alone was to contribute not 104 per cent, as
specified in the 1950 version of the plan, but 280
per cent. Finally, the 1954 standard of living was
to be approximately 50 per cent higher, instead of
the originally set 35 per cent.

The effects of these increased targets on society
in general and the economy in particular were predictable. Agricultural development fell behind, even
basic consumer goods were in short supply, and the
various techniques of forced saving made the individual citizen's life a dreary experience. (Even top
party leaders foresaw the negative effects of the
unrealistically high new targets. Among them, Zoltán
Vas, a former head of the National Planning Office
and a respected economist, was perhaps the most out-
spoken.[3])

The strenuous pace of industrialization could
not be maintained for long. After a considerable
amount of political in-fighting and several changes
in top leadership, the unrealistically high targets

were revised downward in June, 1953. The new goals
aimed at more-balanced economic growth but still
called for a substantial increase in the standard
of living. Although the new version of the plan was
demanding, at least it was not entirely unrealistic.

The New Course, as this period of political and
economic liberalization was called, did not, however,
last very long. Before the end of the plan period,
new political maneuvers started, shifting the balance
of power back to those party leaders who still believed that forced industrialization was a necessity.
Before these party leaders could regain their power,
however, the First Five-Year Plan was completed in
1954. Although total industrial output had increased
158 per cent over the 1949 level, other achievements
fell considerably short of the original and both the
1951 and the 1953 revised expectations.

Heavy industrial production, for example, had
increased only 188 per cent over the 1949 level; this
compared unfavorably with the 1951 specification of
a 280-per-cent increase and that of 215 per cent
specified in the 1953 version of the plan.[4] Although
real wages increased 6 per cent in 1953 and 18 per
cent in 1954, neither the 35-per-cent nor the 50-per-
cent expected increase in the standard of living
materialized. According to official figures, by 1954
the standard of living was 20 per cent lower than at
the beginning of the planning period.[5]

Thus, the First Five-Year Plan ended with mixed
results. Although Hungary did not become an "iron
and steel country," it considerably improved its
industrial capacity. This improvement, however, took
place at the expense of the agricultural sector and
the standard of living of the population.

For the year 1955, only an annual plan was developed. The general objective of the plan was,
again, rapid industrialization at any cost. As a
consequence of uncertainties and sudden changes in
both the political leadership and the planning process
during 1953-54, industrial production rose only 7
per cent in 1955. Considerable increases, however,

were registered in several industries, such as power
generation, oil extraction, and refining.[6]

The Second Five-Year Plan was to be started in
1956. According to official published guidelines,
industrial output was expected to increase 50-52
per cent over the 1955 level. Although heavy industry
continued to be favored over all other sectors of the
economy, emphasis was also put on the exploration of
natural resources and energy sources. Furthermore,
the plan envisioned an extensive division of labor
among the member countries of COMECON (the Council
for Mutual Economic Assistance, founded by the Eastern European socialist countries in 1949). The plan
was never put into effect, however; for the uprising
of October-November, 1956, made its implementation
impossible.

Managerial Environment

Managerial practices and behavior are shaped, to
a large extent, by the environment in which the managerial functions have to be performed.[7] This environment consists of various institutional arrangements,
such as government structure and industrial organization. As pointed out previously, by the start of the
First Five-Year Plan, the Hungarian Working People's
Party was in complete control of the country. This
control was all-pervasive and included the detailed
management of the entire economy.

The basis of all economic activity was the centrally developed plan. Initiation of the plan was
in the hands of the Central Committee of the party,
which "recognized and applied the economic laws of
socialism" to the determination of general plan objectives.[8] Development of specific plan targets was
the responsibility of the National Planning Office.
This office maintained its relationship to the Council
of Ministers through the People's Economic Council
(which was abolished in 1952).

The National Planning Office consisted of general
and industrial departments. The general departments
were charged with the development of comprehensive

financial, labor, and related plans for the entire
economy; whereas the industrial departments had to
draw up specific plans for the different sectors of
the economy. On the next level of authority were
the ministerial general departments, which had the
job of developing comprehensive industry plans. To
these general departments were attached the industrial
departments, or directorates, which represented the
numerous branches within each industry.

The authority relationships below the ministerial
level varied. Some directorates independently managed
day-to-day operations of enterprises under their
jurisdiction, whereas others issued directives through
industrial trusts, usually made up of approximately
four to six enterprises. Under such conditions, the
directorates, in a sense, had to share their authority
with the trusts. Figure 1 illustrates the authority
relationships of the centrally planned Hungarian
economy during 1950-56.

Plan development underwent three different
stages.[9] First, a preliminary plan was prepared,
which included chiefly the general objectives to be
accomplished during the planning period. Second,
a final comprehensive plan was developed for the
entire economy. Third, the comprehensive plan was
broken down into detailed enterprise operating plans,
which served as a blueprint for most managerial decisions.

Throughout all three stages, enterprise managers
were never given a chance to participate. Before the
plan became final, however, they were given an opportunity to develop a counterplan. Through it, managers usually attempted to reduce the officially set
target requirements and, thus, to receive bonuses.
(The bonus system and its managerial implications
will be discussed below.)

The plan permeated every aspect of economic life
both at the national and at the enterprise level. In
addition to the detailed production targets, for example, centrally formulated financial indexes, as

FIGURE 1

Industrial Authority Structure, 1950-56

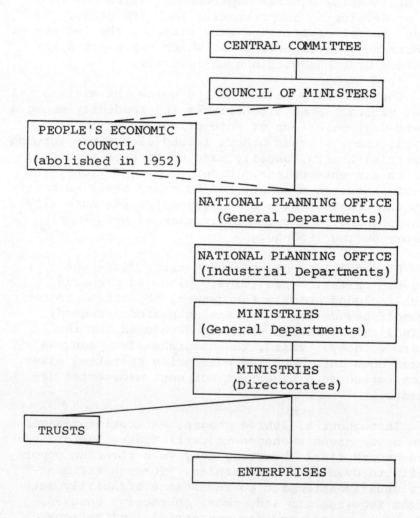

Source: Béla Balassa, The Hungarian Experience in Economic Planning (New Haven: Yale University Press, 1959), p. 57.

well as those of technical development, material
supply, labor cost, and investment renewal, had to
be strictly observed by enterprise managers. According to Balassa, this high degree of centralization
of decision-making authority resulted in a managerial
environment characterized by the following conditions:

1. The dictated targets of the plan pre-
    scribed production of commodities in
    quantitative and qualitative terms.
    They also determined the cost of pro-
    duction.

2. Most of the materials--the important
    ones, without exception--were allocated
    centrally by the authorities.

3. The number of employees in different
    categories, the wage rates, the majority
    of work-norm incentives, and the total
    wage fund were predetermined by the
    central authorities.

4. The various ministries appointed the
    general manager, the chief accountant,
    and chief engineers for all enter-
    prises. The ministries also influenced
    the staffing of more-important middle-
    level managerial positions.

5. The allocation, planning, financing,
    and supervising of investment and re-
    newal decisions were undertaken by the
    National Planning Office, the ministries,
    and the Investment Bank.

6. The various enterprises kept accounts
    with either the National Bank or the
    Investment Bank. All payments, except
    very small ones, had to be made through
    this account. The bank that held the
    enterprise's account also supervised
    its financial operations in general.

7. Foreign trade was carried out through
    state trading companies. Individual

enterprises could not directly engage in export-import activities.

8. Prices throughout the entire economy
were set by the National Planning
Office and the various ministries.

9. The various directorates were responsible for the operation of individual enterprises, in accordance
with the predetermined plan.

10. Enterprise operations were monitored
by the National Control Office, the
Ministry of Finance, the National
Bank, the Investment Bank, and the
various ministries.[10]

Thus, managers were greatly constrained in their
day-to-day decision-making. It would, however, be an
oversimplification to thus argue that management in
those years consisted of little more than the carrying
out of orders issued by higher authorities. Many
intra-enterprise decisions had to be made independently, work schedules had to be set up, workers had
to be assigned to various jobs, discipline had to be
maintained, and interpersonal problems had to be re-
solved.

As in all Eastern European countries, however,
the Hungarian leaders did not consider management a
critical factor of industrialization. (The historical reason for this attitude is probably attributable
to Lenin's belief that management in a socialist
economy would be simple, because such an economy could
be managed as a "single firm.") Although great efforts were undertaken to train a sufficiently large
number of engineers and technicians, the teaching of
management as a discipline was almost entirely ignored.

Enterprise organizational structures were virtually standardized throughout industry. Undoubtedly,
from the point of view of the central authorities,
such standardization was desirable. The officially
designed and administered information system

functioned much better under these organizational
arrangements. Furthermore, standardization enabled
higher-level officials to exercise their functional
authority over enterprise operations in a more-
effective way. These benefits, however, were usually
outweighed by the inefficiencies resulting from an
almost complete lack of adjustment of organizational
structures to specific local needs, operating conditions, differing volumes of activity, and managerial abilities.

The most important qualification for the top
managerial position in an enterprise was political
reliability. Consequently, most general managers
were battle-hardened veterans of the party's past
political struggles. Many of them, however, almost
completely lacked necessary managerial experience
and frequently had no education beyond high school.
True, some of these top managers took their appointments very seriously and attempted to learn the rudi-
ments of industrial management on the job.

Such trial-and-error training, however, amounted
to a very expensive way of learning. Its cost had to
be incurred by society in the form of even more inefficient enterprise operations than were already
necessitated by the complex bureaucracy. Years later,
such political appointments were justified in the
following manner: "During the first period, the
period of developing the foundations of socialism,
political reliability by necessity had to be the most
important managerial selection standard. Expertise,
if considered at all, had to be of secondary importance."[11]

Every industrial enterprise's top managerial
group also included a chief engineer, a chief accountant, and a secretary of the party cell. The chief
engineer, who had reasonably well-defined authority,
had to oversee all matters related to the critical
function of production. The chief accountant was in
charge of the internal accounting system and the
development, as well as the timely submission, of the
many different reports required. Thus, he continually
had to see to it that enterprise operations conformed
to the various centrally issued rules and regulations.

The organizational position of the party secretary was somewhat unclear. Although, officially, he
was not part of the authority structure, his influence was always felt throughout all industrial enterprises. He was authorized by the central party organs to help stimulate better work performance and
to report any activity that could impair enterprise
operations. Thus, for all practical purposes, he was
authorized to circumvent the formal authority structure if necessary. This, however, probably did not
happen too often, because the party secretary's evaluation by higher organs was based on the over-all performance of the enterprise. Consequently, it was in
his own interest to maintain reasonably good relations
with all managers and enterprise employees.

Most middle-level managerial positions were
staffed with engineers. Since the fulfillment of
production targets at almost any cost was the single
most important enterprise objective, it was understandable that engineers were favored over all other
managerial candidates. These engineers, however,
knew very little about the less well-structured aspects of industrial management, such as motivation,
leadership, and general interpersonal relations.

In addition, many engineers were not even well-
trained technicians, because they were products of
the many crash educational programs designed to
alleviate the critical shortage of engineering personnel. After-work study programs were set up to
train workers in engineering skills in three years,
instead of the customary four years. The quality of
these programs varied considerably and depended partially on the ability of the instructors available
and partially on the ability of the students admitted.
Good instructors were in short supply, and the major
admission standard was social-class background rather
than aptitude.

Some middle managers were graduates in law or
economics. Their education included primarily the
study of socialist law, political economy, planning
at the national and enterprise levels, bookkeeping,
and the administrative distribution of raw materials

and finished products throughout the economy. Admission standards to these programs were the same as those in the engineering schools, but the curriculum was generally less advanced.

As a consequence of such educational policies, the quality of middle managers throughout industry varied considerably. The situation was further compounded through the appointment of many politically reliable, but entirely inexperienced, worker-managers with limited education. Many of these appointees were basically intelligent and honest individuals who either tried to learn on the job or did not interfere in the work of professionally better-qualified subordinates.

Some appointees, however, were carried away by the importance of their new positions and, ignoring the dictates of common sense, caused considerable damage to enterprise operations and, thus, to society. As in the case of the incapable, but politically reliable, top managers, the average Hungarian citizen had to pay the cost for the mistakes of the many zealous, but incompetent, middle managers.

Both top- and middle-level managers were motivated through a bonus system tied primarily to the quantity of output produced by the enterprise over the planning period. Since managerial salaries were relatively low, the earning of bonuses was of great importance. (In 1956, the basic monthly pay of an engineer was approximately U.S. $110; that of a middle manager [departmental head], U.S. $120-$140; and that of the general manager of a medium-sized firm, U.S. $170.[12])

The maximum amount of bonus payments possible was quite high. In high-priority industries, such as heavy industry, bonuses could amount to 75 per cent of a basic salary. In low-priority industries, the percentage was somewhat smaller, but, from the point of view of the individual manager, still considerable. Consequently, the majority of managers did everything possible to make sure that bonus payments would be forthcoming.

As pointed out above, bonus payments were initially paid chiefly for the fulfillment of production
targets. Later on, however, fulfillment of profit
plans and time-saving, cost-saving, and other related
efforts could also lead to monetary rewards. The
winning of "socialist work competition" was another
avenue for managers to obtain some extra income. The
rewards for such victories, however, usually were not
too high, and, thus, competition generally was not a
very strong motivating factor.

Administrative personnel, production workers,
and supporting staff were motivated in essentially
three different ways. First, monetary bonuses were
awarded for the fulfillment of individual or group
production targets. (In contrast to production
workers, administrative personnel fared much less
well. Their bonuses tended to be much smaller and
quite irregular.) Bonuses were also paid for indirect
contributions to improved production, such as the
saving of material inputs, the speedy repair of
broken-down equipment, or the development of a technical innovation. Most of these bonuses tended to
be sizable; in high-priority industries--for example,
in heavy industry--they made up a considerable part
of the annual income of most workers.

Managers had a considerable amount of authority
as to how to divide the total bonus funds available
and, at times, even to decide what type of worker
contributions should be rewarded. Occasionally,
however, the payment of bonuses was tied to some
over-all national productivity-increase campaign developed and administered by the central authorities.

Second, employee motivation was based on (as it
is known in U.S. literature) participative management.
To this end, a large number of permanent and temporary
committees were organized in all enterprises. The
membership of these committees usually included representatives of top and middle management; administrative personnel; production workers; and party,
union, and youth organizations. The committees were
expected to deal with almost all aspects of organizational life, and their members participated in, for

example, the evaluation of innovations, the shaping
of enterprise social services, and, at times, even
the settling of interpersonal conflicts. Although,
in most cases, the committees were limited to advis-
ing management, sometimes they acted as decision-
making bodies.

Third, administrative personnel, production
workers, and supporting staff were motivated through
moral persuasion. This involved worker, party, union,
and youth organization meetings, seminars, and con-
ferences. The various types of "socialist work competition" also belonged to this category of motivational techniques. The winners of work competition
sometimes received special bonuses; at other times,
awards were limited to intrinsic rewards, such as
the title of "outstanding worker" or "hero of socialist work competition."

Managerial Problems

Under the conditions described above, industrial
management in Hungary was not a simple task. True,
the various managerial functions were performed within
very narrow limits set by the central authorities;
however, managers had to be extremely flexible, imaginative, and even cunning to guide their enterprises
successfully through the maze of complex and detailed
rules and regulations representing these limits.

The basic managerial problem of the centralized
Hungarian economic system was the great disparity
between managerial authority and responsibility. Such
disparity occurs even in the best-managed organizations. Thus, it is not the phenomenon itself, but
the degree to which it occurs, that is critical.
According to good management practice, a manager
should always be given enough authority to perform
the task for whose accomplishment he is responsible.

Under the centralized planning system, the authority given to Hungarian managers never even approxi-
mated the responsibility that higher authorities ex-
tracted from them. Although managers were responsible
for the fulfillment of the centrally developed plan

targets, they were never given authority over most
of those activities that were critical to the fulfillment of these targets. Such authority was retained by the various directorates and ministries,
as well as by the National Planning Office.

To reduce this disparity to an acceptable level,
managers had to resort to all kinds of legal, quasi-
legal, and even illegal practices. The most frequently used legal practice involved the counterplan.
As mentioned earlier, after the central authorities
broke down the various comprehensive plans into enterprise operating plans, managers were given an opportunity to respond to the officially set targets
through the counterplan.

In this, managers attempted to revise the official targets downward to be able to fulfill the operating plans better and, thus, to receive bonuses.
Higher authorities understood this practice and were
aware of its implications. Consequently, in many
cases, they set the initial targets much higher than
they would otherwise have done. Targets set in
counterplans usually resulted in protracted bargaining
processes involving a great deal of time and effort.

The quasi-legal and illegal managerial practices
were mostly related to the material-supply system.
All raw materials, semifinished goods, and other production inputs were allocated to individual enterprises by the central authorities. Under the best
of conditions, such an allocation scheme tends to be
slow and undependable. In Hungary, in addition to
these undesirable characteristics, it also resulted
in large-scale managerial dishonesty.

Managers knew that their material inputs were
the production outputs of other enterprises operating
on the basis of a centrally developed plan and under
constraints similar to their own. They also understood that the material resources of the country were
overcommitted. Consequently, they realized that deliveries of needed materials were, at best, undependable and, at worst, not forthcoming at all. To build

up enough organizational reserves of the most-important inputs, they padded their material-supply requests. Since this was done in almost all industrial enterprises, the shortages caused by the initial over-commitment of material resources were severely amplified.

The padding of material-supply requests was recognized by the central authorities. The number of enterprises involved, however, was so large that it was impossible to eliminate, or even reduce, this practice to an acceptable level. Frequently, managers also resorted to the use of personal contacts, informal interenterprise barter deals, and, sometimes, even outright bribery to obtain the necessary materials. Unofficial contact men were retained by many managers; these so-called pushers had good contacts and, for a sizable fee, were willing to help enterprises get necessary supplies.

In retrospect, it is interesting that, although most of these practices were quite well known at the time, not too many managers were charged with violation of material-supply regulations. It appears that, within certain limits, the central authorities tended to tolerate such practices, because, frequently, they were the only means available to managers to forestall a complete breakdown in enterprise operations.

Despite the tendency of the central authorities to condone such practices and despite their earnest efforts to keep enterprises supplied with the needed material inputs, serious problems and breakdowns did occur. Balassa summed up the effects of the unsatisfactory material-supply system on enterprise operations as follows:

1. Enterprises frequently shut down for various lengths of time because of late or no supply deliveries.

2. Machines frequently had to be retooled because of the varying quality of material inputs supplied.

3. Materials were cross-hauled from one
    enterprise to another to prevent sud-
    den breakdowns in production.

4. In general, materials were wasted.

5. Product quality deteriorated, pri-
    marily because, when the necessary
    materials were not available, mana-
    gers were frequently forced to use
    poorer substitutes.[13]

These and related problems forced managers to
falsify records also. This was probably done in some
form and at some time in all enterprises. It usually
involved all top managers and frequently was done by
the chief accountant personally. Interestingly
enough, as in the case of material-supply regulation
violations, not too many managers were charged with
the willful distortion of official records and reports.
Consequently, in most cases, the false information
entered the over-all information system without any
difficulty and continued to mislead decision-makers
at successively higher levels.

As a consequence of the inadequate material-
supply system, occasional changes in production assignments, planning errors, and various types of
intra-enterprise problems, managers frequently had
to resort to "storming practices" to meet production
target dates. This involved the concerted efforts
of all employees and tended to develop into a sort
of mad rush, during which all other enterprise problems were temporarily shelved. In most cases, the
target dates were met, the products were delivered,
and, thus, the bonuses were forthcoming. Invariably,
however, this practice resulted in poor-quality
products, industrial accidents, and other undesirable
side effects. For example, although the delivery
deadline was met, the receiving enterprise or marketing organization may have needed delivery much sooner.

The desire to maximize bonus income over the
long run also forced managers to try to minimize

the risk involved in all managerial decisions. Consequently, as a rule, they shunned general technological and specific product innovations. Although the
central authorities assigned a great deal of importance to innovations, most managers did little more
than pay lip service to the idea. Most of them were
not willing to risk the relatively safe production
bonuses for the sake of experimenting with new equipment or new product or process ideas.

This is not to say that no technological innovations or new product ideas were generated. Many
Hungarian engineers, technicians, and workers had
submitted outstanding ideas for consideration. Many
of these were accepted and implemented. In relation
to the number of opportunities and needs, however,
the number of innovations submitted, tried, accepted,
and implemented was relatively small.

Managers frequently encountered problems in
motivating employees. From a manager's point of
view, the overfulfillment of individual or group plan
targets was generally desirable, but, sometimes, managerial and worker interests clashed on this point.
The managers recognized that the consistent overful-
filling of plan targets could easily lead to increased
plan targets the next time around. This, in turn,
could make it more difficult to fulfill a new enterprise plan and, consequently, to obtain the much-
desired bonus payments.

Also, the attendance by managers at the various
enterprise committee meetings designed to generate
employee participation in management occasionally
created problems. These committee meetings, as they
do everywhere, consumed an inordinate amount of pre-
cious managerial time. As pointed out above, the
committees acted chiefly in an advisory capacity.
Very seldom did they actually engage in decision-
making. Thus, managers, hard pressed by the problems
of making day-to-day operational decisions, frequently
had to participate in perhaps interesting, but, in
the short run, unproductive, deliberations. This
problem was further compounded by the usually compulsory and frequent political mass meetings or

ideological seminars in which managers had to play
an active role in order to set a good example for
their employees.

THE MANAGER AND THE ECONOMY,
1957-67

The uprising during Autumn, 1956, caused considerable damage to the Hungarian economy. Various
loans and grants, including a 3 billion foreign-
exchange forint loan from other socialist countries,
were necessary to restore the economy.[14] The loans
and grants notwithstanding, the economic situation
in 1957 was very serious. Excessive wage increases
created strong inflationary pressures. By August,
1957, the general price level was 20 per cent higher
than in 1956. Exports were considerably lower and
imports higher than during the previous years. Labor
discipline was low, and pilferage became almost
fashionable.[15] Nevertheless, by the end of 1957,
total industrial output was approximately 17 per cent
higher than during 1956, and, under the existing conditions, this was a modest success.

In 1958, the Second Three-Year Plan was started.
It called for a general reconstruction of the torn
economy. Strong efforts were undertaken to improve
labor discipline. "Socialist work competition" became widespread, and, at one point, approximately
19,000 brigades, or approximately 13 per cent of the
total industrial-labor force, participated in an
all-out effort to increase productivity.[16] These
concerted efforts led to some improvements. According to reports of the Central Statistical Office, by
1960, industrial output had increased 40 per cent
over the 1957 level, productivity was up 20 per cent,
and the balance of trade was favorable. Thus, by the
end of the plan period, the major economic problems
caused by the 1956 events had been corrected.

The Second Five-Year Plan (1961-65) was based
on a sober approach and the experiences of the previous decade. The general objective of the plan was
to "finish building the foundations of socialism"

and to "start building the developed socialist
society."17   More specifically, it called for a considerable increase in labor productivity and improvement of industrial technology and product quality.
To this end, the plan specified the replacement of
old industrial equipment and machinery, as well as
the building of more than 100 modern industrial
plants.

Results of the plan were respectable, although
somewhat disappointing. National income rose only
25 per cent, instead of the planned 36 per cent.
Industrial productivity increased 27 per cent, instead of 33 per cent.18   Although total investment
was slightly higher than planned, technological development, in general, fell short of the plan's
target. The balance-of-payments situation became
steadily more critical; the deficit accumulated between 1957 and 1965 totaled 7 billion foreign-exchange
forints or more than U.S. $0.5 billion.

The general objectives of the Third Five-Year
Plan (1966-70), which included three years (1968-70)
of the New Economic Mechanism (NEM), were to modernize
the structure of Hungarian industry and to increase
the energy-producing base of the economy. The two
pre-reform years, 1966 and 1967, resulted in a reasonably satisfactory economic performance.19   National
income rose 7.8 per cent in 1966 and 8.1 per cent in
1967, and investments were 9.9 per cent and 21.7 per
cent higher, respectively, than during the previous
years.

Total industrial output grew 6.7 per cent in
1966 and 8.7 per cent in 1967, with the chemical,
construction, and engineering industries performing
especially well. Increases in labor productivity,
however, were disappointing in both years and fell
below expectations. The 1966 balance of payments
closed with a 327 million foreign-exchange forint
surplus, whereas the 1967 balance showed an 870 million foreign-exchange forint deficit, chiefly because
of a considerable increase in imports from nonsocialist countries.

Managerial Environment

The gradual switch from a strategy of forced industrialization to one of more-balanced economic growth during 1957-67 was accompanied by a partial restructuring of the managerial environment. The first major step in this direction was the slow elimination of industrial directorates and the merging of many industrial enterprises into trusts. The objective of the reorganization was a limited decentralization of authority to the enterprise level.

By the end of 1963, more than 600 industrial enterprises were merged into about 200 new units, and, of the approximately sixty industrial directorates, more than thirty were abolished. The newly merged enterprises were combined into trusts possessing considerable authority. They were empowered to determine the size of wage funds, to allocate investments, and to assign production targets to enterprises under their jurisdiction. Their authority, however, was not absolute; on most issues, the ministries still exercised a veto.

In 1957, the first profit-sharing scheme was developed. It authorized managers to pay bonuses out of profit equal to the wages earned over a certain number of working days if average annual production costs had been reduced at least 3 per cent. In 1962, the basic wage and salary structure was revised, and a technical innovation bonus system was introduced. These measures enabled managers to set basic wages and salaries in a more flexible manner and to reward outstanding technical innovations independent of short-term production results.

In 1959, the wholesale price structure was reformed. In general, prices were increased both to reflect true scarcity values and to conform to existing industrial cost structures better. Several major industrial enterprises were permitted to conduct their foreign-trade relations independently. Other enterprises engaged in foreign trade were allowed to retain a certain amount of hard-currency earnings to obtain materials and equipment for modernization purposes.

Thus, for the first time, industrial enterprises had some incentive to increase exports on a continuous basis.

In 1964, a unique measure for an Eastern European socialist country was introduced. Industrial enterprises were instructed to pay a 5-per-cent interest rate on gross fixed and variable capital. (Gross fixed capital included buildings and machines, but not land. Variable capital was defined as raw materials, tools, fuel, and semifinished and finished products.) This was intended to stimulate the better use of machines, to promote rational investment decisions, to reduce the hoarding of materials, and to improve product quality. (The 5-per-cent interest rate on the inventory of finished products amounted to a very serious penalty if the products were unsalable.)

Although higher authorities continued to appoint top, and even some middle, managers during 1960-64, the standards of managerial selection were substantially changed. Educational background and professional competence were considered to be almost as important qualifications as were political reliability and party membership. Throughout the 1957-67 period, the number of specific directives issued by higher authorities was reduced. Consequently, managers had more freedom in selecting suppliers, locating consumers, and hiring employees.

Several major aspects of the pre-1957 managerial environment, however, were little affected by the changes. The rigid and artificial consumer price structure, for example, was maintained in essentially the same form under the supervision of a newly established (in 1957) Office of Price Control. Methods of financing and techniques of over-all enterprise control underwent inconsequential revisions. Thus, although the managerial environment underwent some changes during the decade preceding the 1968 reform, these changes were of a rather limited nature and did not affect the fundamental characteristics of the centralized planning system as described.

Managerial Problems

As a consequence of only a partial restructuring of the environment during 1957-67, managers continued to have problems. They still had to be flexible, imaginative, and cunning. The great disparity between managerial authority and responsibility was not re-duced. On the contrary, some of the partial changes in the managerial environment actually widened the gap. The nature of some of the problems, however, was different.

The reduction in the number of centrally issued directives initially promised more managerial author-ity and flexibility. Managers, however, soon dis-covered that this increase in authority and flexi-bility worked to their disadvantage. Fewer directives also meant the loss of centrally appointed suppliers and consumers. At the same time, truly free trade between enterprises, suppliers, and consumers did not exist. Consequently, most industrial managers sud-denly found that partially because of the lack of directives and partially because of the lack of free trade, they had great difficulties obtaining material supplies and selling the products manufactured.

Thus, industrial managers were caught between two half measures that they could not change or even influence for the better. To assure the continued operation of their enterprises, they again had to resort to various quasi-legal and illegal practices. Many managers once more obtained material supplies through "pushers," and, after a while, these practices became so widespread that higher authorities, recog-nizing the problem, again started issuing more and more specific directives.

The appointment of "experts" to replace dedicated party members in important managerial positions also created several intra-organizational problems.[20] Over the years, the old-guard managers tended to build up a loyal following of employees who had obtained their positions through the managers. Such employees were now afraid that they could lose their jobs. Conse-quently, the new experts were frequently resented and, on occasion, their orders were quietly sabotaged.

With the passage of time, however, this problem slowly
tended to take care of itself through voluntary resig-
nations, transfers, and natural attrition. Nevertheless, in the meantime, the atmosphere of many enterprises was considerably poisoned.

The low level of employee discipline and labor
productivity during 1957-67 presented industrial managers with another set of serious problems. (According
to official figures, the labor-productivity index in
Hungary during the early 1960's was 141 [1950 = 100].
In contrast to this, it was 174 in Bulgaria, 197 in
Rumania, and 209 in the German Democratic Republic.[21])
The newly introduced profit-sharing plan did not entirely fulfill management's expectations because it
did not motivate employees to improve their discipline
and over-all performance. Very frequently, bonus payments were made illegally, and, after a while, most
employees began to look upon them as a regular part
of their income. (Bonus payments could be made only
if enterprise production costs were reduced by at
least 3 per cent over the profit-plan period. Many
managers, however, simply falsified enterprise cost
records, thus making such payments possible.)

In 1960, to increase labor productivity, higher
authorities decided to increase work norms considerably throughout industry. Managers were instructed
to develop new norms on the basis of detailed studies
of enterprise conditions. The measure was very un-
popular, and enterprise managers faced a very serious
dilemma in that they could either ignore the orders
issued by the central authorities or further reduce
labor discipline and morale by rigidly setting higher
and, thus, more demanding work norms.

Within a short period of time, a great deal of
tension had built up in most industrial enterprises.
Some managers quite openly took the side of the
workers and resisted the government's demands for
higher norms.[22] Some managers falsified records
and, in general, did everything possible to undermine
the new directives.[23] Other managers set the new
norms without even trying to consult their employees.
In many enterprises, workers were forced to abide by
the arbitrarily set norms in no uncertain terms.[24]

Higher authorities, however, very soon recognized that norms were evaded or too aggressively enforced. They put a great deal of pressure on managers to improve their own performance and, thus, to set a good example for their employees.[25] Furthermore, managers were instructed to consult workers before setting the norms and, in general, to use a more employee-centered style of management.

During the years immediately preceeding the introduction of a new economic system in 1968, the nature of these managerial problems did not substantially change. Managers continued to be handicapped by rules and regulations, and they never possessed enough authority to fulfill all their responsibilities consistently. Supply problems persisted, sales were difficult, and labor productivity remained relatively low. The various types of incentive plans did not seem to motivate employees to improve their performance significantly, and, in general, managers could not escape the continuous tutelage of higher authorities. The increasing recognition by higher authorities of management as a critical factor of industrialization nevertheless seemed to promise a better future. But managers had to wait until after January 1, 1968, to benefit from this attitude change.

CONCLUDING REMARKS

Much has been written about the strategies of industrialization as developed and applied in the Soviet Union and the other Eastern European socialist countries.[26] Most writers acknowledge that the impressive growth rates experienced by these countries during the early 1950's could not have been achieved without the consistent application of the centralized planning system. At the same time, these writers always point out the inherent limitations of such a system in countries less well endowed with natural resources than is the Soviet Union. Several authors emphasize the high cost that the people had to pay for these achievements in terms of a relatively low standard of living and a regimented way of life.

The literature dealing with the Hungarian experience follows the same lines.[27] Most authors agree that although Hungary did not become an "iron and steel" country it has, in a relatively short period of time, considerably increased its industrial base. In most of this literature, however, it is emphasized that the blind acceptance of the Soviet model was a mistake, because Hungary never possessed the resources necessary to permit forced industrialization without substantial damage to its economy and people.[28]

When the limited changes implemented during the early 1960's could not correct the deficiencies of the central planning system, the Hungarian leaders recognized that, in the long run, only a complete reform could guarantee a well-balanced economy and, thus, a considerably higher standard of living. The road leading to this recognition was not an easy one. It called for a considerable amount of political and moral courage, because the introduction of a complete reform necessitated a sharp break with economic and managerial beliefs and practices embedded in the doctrinaire ideology of the past.

NOTES

1. See Társadalmi Szemle (Social Review), No. 3 (1951), pp. 131-51.

2. The data presented here are from Béla Balassa, The Hungarian Experience in Economic Planning (New Haven, Conn.: Yale University Press, 1959), pp. 31-32; and Ernst C. Helmreich, Hungary (New York: Frederick A. Praeger, 1957), pp. 294-95.

3. Balassa, The Hungarian Experience, p. 32.

4. Helmreich, Hungary, p. 295.

5. Ivan T. Berend, "The Historical Background of the Recent Economic Reforms in East Europe (The Hungarian Experience)," East European Quarterly, No. 3 (September, 1963), p. 83.

6.   Helmreich, Hungary, p. 296.

7.   For a discussion of the relationship between managerial performance and the environment, see Richard N. Farmer and Barry M. Richman, Comparative Management and Economic Progress (Homewood, Ill.: Richard D. Irwin, 1965).

8.   Balassa, The Hungarian Experience, p. 56.

9.   Ibid., p. 58.

10.   Ibid., pp. 124-25.

11.   Rezsö Nyers, "Utunk, Céljaink, Elveink--Egy Negyedszázad Tükrében" (Our Road, Objectives and Principles in the Mirror of a Quarter Century), Gazdaság, April, 1970, p. 27.

12.   Balassa, The Hungarian Experience, p. 133.

13.   Ibid., pp. 77-78.

14.   Belpolitikai Szemle (Review of Domestic Politics), June 18, 1958, p. 2.

15.   Népakarat (People's Will), November 12, 1957, p. 3.

16.   Népszava (People's Word), January 4, 1961, p. 2.

17.   Magyar Közlöny (Hungarian Gazette), October 17, 1961, p. 544.

18.   Népszabadság, (People's Freedom), April 10, 1966, p. 2.

19.   All data are based on Statisztikai Évkönyv 1969 (Statistical Yearbook 1969) (Budapest: Központi Statisztikai Hivatal, 1970).

20.   Népszabadság, June 16, 1963, p. 2, and July 13, 1963, p. 3.

21. _Magyar Nemzet_ (Hungarian Nation), July 17, 1962, p. 2.

22. _Népszabadság_, September 7, 1960, p. 2.

23. _Ibid._, November 26, 1961, p. 2.

24. _Ibid._, June 14, 1961, p. 2, and June 6, 1962, p. 3.

25. _Ibid._, October 10, 1962, p. 3.

26. See, for example, Nicholas Spulber, _The Economics of Communist Eastern Europe_ (Cambridge, Mass.: The M.I.T. Press, 1957); Gregory Grossman, ed., _Value and Plan, Economic Calculation and Organization in Eastern Europe_ (Berkeley: University of California Press, 1960); and Nicholas Spulber, _Socialist Management and Planning_ (Bloomington: Indiana University Press, 1971).

27. Balassa, _The Hungarian Experience_; Janos Kornai, _Overcentralization in Economic Administration, A Critical Analysis Based on Experience in Hungarian Light Industry_ (New York: Oxford University Press, 1959); Berend, "The Historical Background"; and Ferenc Jánossy, "The Origins of Contradictions in Our Economy and the Path to Their Solution," _Eastern European Economics_, Summer, 1970.

28. Jánossy, "The Origins of Contradictions," pp. 370-74.

2

THE
REFORM

The reform, introduced on January 1, 1968, had
been carefully prepared. As early as December, 1964,
the Central Committee of the Hungarian Working People's Party had decided to start large-scale discussions concerning the possibility of adopting a new
economic system. To this end, study groups composed
of economic and other experts were formed. The more
than 100 members of these groups were officially encouraged to develop their ideas freely and to submit
them for public debate. Soon, the various mass media
were full of proposals, counterproposals, and even
strong criticism of past and current economic policies.

In November, 1965, the Central Committee announced a decision to support those experts who had
recommended a complete restructuring of the economic
system.[1] This ended the debates concerning the de-
sirability of the reform. On May 7, 1966, the Central
Committee passed a resolution to introduce the reform
under the title of the New Economic Mechanism. On
November 24, 1967, the Central Committee officially
authorized NEM's implementation as of January 1,
1968.[2]

GENERAL BACKGROUND

Objectives of the reform were summed up by the
official Hungarian Government newspaper in the

33

following manner: "The main purpose of the reform
is to free our economy of its wearisome and rigid
features, to develop its superiority over the capitalist system, to establish harmony with objective
economic laws, and to stimulate further development."[3]
Rezsö Nyers, secretary of the Central Committee and
chairman of its Economic Policy Committee, emphasized
in several official statements and publications that
NEM was not just a partial revision of the existing
economic order but a fundamental and irreversible
reform of the entire economy.

As such, NEM is based on the proposition that,
within the limits of the socialist economic framework,
a relatively high degree of decentralization of economic decision-making authority to the enterprise
level, together with utilization of the market mechanism, is the only way to revitalize the stagnating
Hungarian economy and, thus, to provide a better
future for the people. Thus, the reform introduced
the socialist market economy into Hungary. This
economy, although not as liberal as that of Yugoslavia, is unique in Eastern Europe. It takes into consideration Hungarian history, culture, emotional
experience, and mental attitudes. As such, it tends
to serve as a testing ground for many new ideas here-
tofore unknown in the Eastern European socialist
economies.

It is important to point out, however, that the
new policies were made within the framework of the
political and economic teachings of Marx and Lenin
and that they in no way signal a return to capitalism
or even to a mixed economy. Nevertheless, the reform
led to the adoption of several economic principles
("objective economic laws") long known and applied
in capitalist economies of the world. This resulted
in changes in the role of central planning and led
to the introduction of the market place, competition,
and profit into Hungary's economic system.

Role of Central Planning

The Hungarian economy is still centrally planned;
and major economic, social, and cultural objectives

continue to be defined in official fifteen- and five-year plans. These plans also establish guidelines for the distribution of national income, the general competitive conditions to exist in the market place, and the course of international trade relations. Plan objectives, however, are no longer realized through specific enterprise operating targets and detailed administrative directives.

The economy, in general, and individual enterprises, in particular, are influenced toward desired objectives through the selective use of "economic regulators," such as taxation, credit policies, and foreign-exchange allocations. The National Bank, the Investment Bank, the National Materials and Price Office, and the Ministry of Foreign Trade are some of the institutions through which the economic regulators are administered.

The central plans, therefore, are no longer compulsory for individual enterprises. Managers, however, are strongly advised to use the plans as basic premises in the development of their enterprise plans. Under no circumstances, however, does the government want to coerce managers to follow the central plan at any cost. As a consequence, it is possible that, in the short run, the general conditions in the economy will deviate from conditions prescribed in the central plan. Depending on the particular situation, this can lead to a change in the role of certain economic regulators, modification of the central plan, or acceptance of the new conditions, such decisions being basically of a political nature.

Participation in the development of central plans in Hungary is institutionalized for almost all segments of society. Throughout the entire planning process, the National Planning Office stays in close touch with several advisory committees. These committees--for example, the Committee on Labor and the Standard of Living, the Committee on Territorial Development, and the Committee on Economic Issues--represent a highly diversified group of individuals who are expected to study public needs, desires, and opinions continuously and carefully. They are also

expected to publish their ideas, proposals, and even
criticisms in popular, professional, and academic
publications in order to generate discussion of the
issues involved.

Under such conditions, the new role of the central plan in Hungary is not very much different from
the role that "Le Plan" plays in France. In both
countries, the general long-range objectives include
a high rate of economic growth, relatively stable
employment, and technological advancements. Also,
the plans in both countries convey to managers a
priority list of development objectives and define
the various means through which such objectives can
best be accomplished. Furthermore, managerial, professional, and special-interest groups are asked to
participate in the planning process through the
presentation of ideas, proposals, and constructive
criticism.

In Hungary, these new features contrast sharply
with those of the past. Before 1968, central plans
were developed by the key leadership of the party,
together with a few technocrats whose main concern
was the ideological correctness of objectives and the
planning process itself. (This is not to say that
political considerations are not important any more.
Far from it, they are still very important; however,
they are no longer the sole consideration.)

The new planners represent a varied group of
well-educated party technocrats and well-trained
specialists in econometrics, operations research,
and the social sciences. Human qualities, such as
imagination and daring, which were suspect in planners in the past, are now at a premium. Consequently,
central planning in Hungary is no longer a coercive
process based on arbitrary decisions and utopian objectives. Under the new economic system, it is a
guiding process based on rational decisions and realistic objectives.

Role of Market Place and Competition

Hungary's new market place serves as a meeting
ground for sellers and buyers, who are free to choose

their trading partners. Centrally issued compulsory delivery agreements no longer specify the trading contacts of enterprises, although they can enter into such agreements among themselves. The market place is expected to stimulate technological inventions and accelerate economic growth, because it puts higher values on products that are more up-to-date, more efficient, and more fashionable. It should also provide central planners with information as to what measures they have to take to balance the economy better. Finally, through purchase decisions, the market place is designated to help in the reduction of unnecessary labor and, thus, to improve industrial efficiency.

The nature and limits of competition are defined by the special characteristics of the new market place, which not only performs a regulatory function but is itself regulated. Within general guidelines of the plan, the reactivated market place is organized and regulated by the central authorities through various direct and indirect means, such as administrative orders (issued only in exceptional cases), the price system, and economic regulators. For example, the central authorities plan the aggregate purchasing power of the population, oversee pricing practices, allocate foreign exchange, and, if necessary, redefine enterprise activities. The regulations are not rigid and permit a certain amount of flexibility. Whenever plan guidelines and market developments do not coincide, adjustments in both the plan and the market place are possible.

Although competition is permitted to cause some changes in the market place and in the various industries, the large-scale elimination of enterprises and major industrial regroupings are prevented. Enterprises that incur serious losses as a result of competition can be financially aided, merged, or reorganized. Such action is taken on the basis of detailed economic studies and in the interest of long-range plan objectives.

Several factors, including high-investment requirements, economies of scale, and past politico-economic decisions, make over-all competitive

participation in the domestic market place impossible.
Some major enterprises--such as truck, tractor, and
bus manufacturing, as well as a few engineering en-
terprises--enjoy a quasi-monopoly position in production. Care is taken, however, to prevent any of
these enterprises from developing an additional monopoly in the distribution of their products. Furthermore, whenever possible, import competition is
encouraged to weaken their strong position, although
current foreign-exchange shortages considerably limit
such use of imports.

Role of Profit

The reintroduction of the market place and competition resulted in the acceptance of profit as the
most important enterprise success indicator. Despite
certain limitations on the use of profit to judge
enterprise operations--for example, the sellers' market conditions, the restrictions on competition, and
continued regulation of prices--the reformers believe
that, together with less-tangible standards, such as
the rate of technical invention and social contributions, profit is still the best comprehensive indicator of enterprise performance.

A large part of the profit earned is taxed away
by the central authorities. The remainder is divided
among the enterprise's development, sharing, and reserve funds. The sharing fund is taxed progressively
in relation to the annual wage bill. After tax de-
ductions, 10 per cent of this fund has to be put in
the reserve fund. The remaining amount has to cover
social services provided by the enterprise, annual
wage increases, and the incentive payments to managers
and employees on the basis of the profit-sharing
classification scheme. The development fund is taxed
60 per cent on the average. After deduction of taxes,
10 per cent of this fund has to be put into the reserve fund. The remainder is supplemented through
depreciation and possible special government appropri-
ations. The fund can be used by management for investment purposes.

The reserve fund, made up of 10 per cent annual
contributions from the development and sharing funds,

has to be maintained at a level equal to 8 per cent
of the annual wage bill plus 1.5 per cent of the
actual gross value of fixed and variable assets
(capital). It can be used to cover actual losses
and to complement the development and sharing funds.
Amounts withdrawn for such purpose, however, must be
repaid within an officially set time period. Figure
2 shows the relationship between profit and the various enterprise funds.

NEW MANAGERIAL ENVIRONMENT

The reform substantially changed the formerly
rigid and complex managerial environment. (The following discussion presents the managerial environment
as of January 1, 1968; subsequent changes are not included here.) The role of the central authorities
was redefined, and, with a few exceptions, most economic decision-making authority was decentralized to
the enterprise level.

Although the party continues to have a decisive
role in economic policy-making, it no longer bases
all economic decisions on political considerations
alone. Many party and government leaders, such as
Rezsö Nyers and Jenö Fock, are accomplished economic
experts and administrators. (Reszö Nyers was one of
the major architects of the reform. The prime minister, Jenö Fock, served several years as the president
of the Economic Committee before becoming head of the
government.) Other authorities make extensive use of
expert economic advice in their daily work. As a
result, the new relationships among party organs,
government agencies, and enterprise managers tend to
be much more flexible and pragmatic than in the past.

The over-all industrial authority structure under
NEM is illustrated in Figure 3. The Central Committee
of the Hungarian Working People's Party and the Council of Ministers continue as the supreme economic
authority of the country. The Council of Ministers
is supported in its work by the Economic Committee,
which includes the ministers in charge of economic,
industrial, and agricultural affairs.

FIGURE 2

Distribution of Profit Among Enterprise Funds

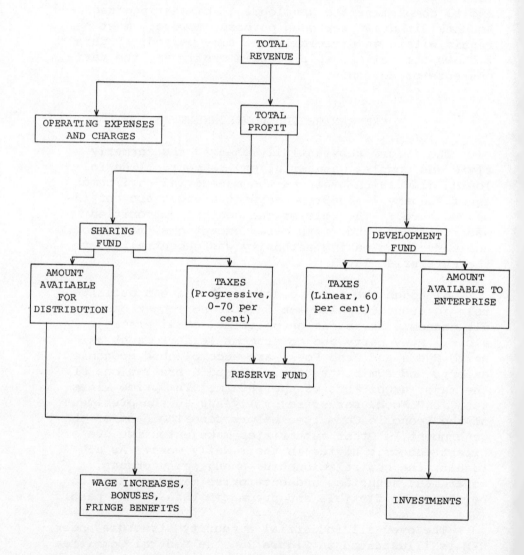

FIGURE 3

New Industrial Authority Structure, 1968

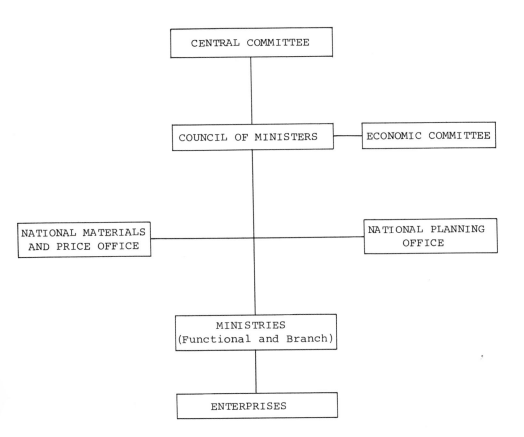

The National Planning Office lost a great deal
of its former authority, although it still organizes
and directs development of the various short-, medium-,
and long-term plans for the entire economy. These
plans are compulsory only for state administrative
bodies; individual enterprises are no longer bound
by them. In its new role, the National Planning
Office acts chiefly as a planner and coordinator of
over-all economic development. For example, it
studies economic conditions and coordinates the use
of the economic regulators administered by the different functional ministries. It also evaluates
technical and economic development proposals submitted
by the National Board of Technical Development (essentially a study group dealing with technical and economic development issues), the banks, the ministries,
and the enterprises.

The functional authority of the National Planning
Office is limited to matters associated with the development of plans. It reports all its activities
to the Council of Ministers and, if called upon, ad-
vises the same on issues of economic policy and planning. Development and maintenance of equilibria in
macroeconomic balances, such as the balance of consumer goods and industrial products, is the shared
responsibility of the National Planning Office and
the National Materials and Price Office. (The head
of the National Materials and Price Office, Béla
Csikós-Nagy, is one of the most respected experts
on pricing in the socialist world.)

Participation of the various ministries and
agencies in the balancing process is ensured through
the Interministerial Committee for Materials and
Prices. The ultimate decision-making authority in
regulating trade and pricing of selected commodities,
however, rests with the government, which, through
the National Materials and Price Office, formulates
and administers such regulation. Consequently, this
office is one of the most important and most powerful
economic agencies in Hungary.

The ministries are divided into two different
groups. The functional ministries--for example, the

Ministry of Labor and the Ministry of Finance--super-
vise all branches of the economy through the administration of economic regulators. They have no direct
supervisory authority over branch ministries or enterprise operations.

The branch ministries--for example, the Ministries of Heavy Industry, of Light Industry, of Domestic Trade, and of Metallurgy and Engineering--are the
supervisory agencies in their respective branches of
industry. They are responsible for the development
and effective administration of their branches according to the central plan guidelines. Their supervisory
authority includes the power to start new enterprises,
to redefine enterprise activities, to appoint and
dismiss top enterprise managers, to evaluate and audit
enterprise performance, and, if in the national interest, to issue specific operational instructions to
enterprise managers. Such directives, however, can
be issued only in exceptional cases.

Similar supervisory authority is retained by
certain local (town and county) councils over public
utilities and industrial, construction, and trade
enterprises. In 1968, however, such enterprises
represented only about 5 per cent of Hungarian industry.[4] Thus, the role of local councils is less
important than is that of the branch ministries.

The relationship between the supervisory branch
ministries or the local councils, on the one hand,
and the individual enterprises, on the other hand,
is usually a direct one. In exceptional cases, however, the supervisory agencies can maintain their
relationship to individual enterprises through trusts
or other types of industrial associations.

It is necessary to point out, however, that
trusts are no longer an important means of industrial
organization. Under NEM, they are economic units
without the intermediate supervisory authority that
they had in the past. Furthermore, most trusts formed
during the pre-reform years were dissolved, and the
start of new ones required the Economic Committee's
permission. Since trusts are considered monopolistic

organizations that tend to reduce competition in the
market place, such permission is not easy to obtain.
Nevertheless, as a result of economic efficiency
considerations, a limited number of vertical and even
horizontal trust formations do exist.

Within this general organizational framework, the
individual enterprise represents a legal entity, and
its top manager has the authority to make or delegate
independent decisions in the following areas:

1. Enterprise planning

2. Hiring, promotion, transfer, and discharge of employees

3. Technological development

4. Credit policies

5. Contractual arrangements and supplies

6. Product, product-mix, and sales policies

7. Self-financed investments

8. Development of enterprise balance sheets

9. Development and joining of enterprise
   associations

10. Enterprise organizational structures

11. Enterprise operating procedures.[5]

Naturally, decisions in all of these areas have to be
made within the existing legal framework, such as the
Labor Code, and in line with the various economic
regulators controlled by the central authorities.

Material-Supply System

The reform led to the abolishment of the central
material-supply system and the elimination of compulsory delivery contracts between individual enterprises.

(If the over-all national interest requires it, however, the Central Court of Arbitration has the authority to direct enterprises to enter into such contracts.) With few exceptions, the new material-supply system is based on free interenterprise trade in the market place.

To expedite the movement of material supplies from producers to intermediary users, specialized "trading enterprises" were created. These are essentially independent wholesalers, who have the same rights and duties as manufacturing industrial enterprises. Their profits are generated by the trade margin, and they pay the same charge on assets and the same interest rate on capital borrowed from the banks. They are permitted to buy, at their own risk, directly from foreign-trade enterprises and can, on occasion, act as commission agents. They cannot, however, be appointed exclusive representatives.

The limitations imposed upon free trade in material supplies are necessary to maintain the required equilibria in the various macroeconomic balances. The limitations are centrally planned and are administered by the National Materials and Price Office. Most are of a transitional nature, although it is not clear when they will be abolished. The most severe form of limitation is the quota used for products for which demand and supply equilibrium cannot be safeguarded through the use of economic regulators. During the first year of the reform, agricultural products, such as meat and grain, were allocated on this basis.

Also, in certain cases, compulsory delivery contracts have to be negotiated. These are chiefly applicable to the centrally allocated products (meat and grain) and items that are important for national defense purposes. Compulsory channels of distribution also limit free trade in material supplies. Single agencies are appointed as exclusive distributors of selected products. The products so controlled are basic food items and goods that have to be made available to users at officially fixed prices.

Price System

Increased reliance on the market place and on competition called for a substantial restructuring of the price system. In developing the new system, the reformers considered the average cost of production, demand conditions in domestic and foreign markets, and government preferences in terms of desirable social and economic objectives.

The average cost of production, based on enterprise cost calculations, includes materials, wages, a 25-per-cent payroll tax, depreciation, and a 5-percent charge on the gross value of fixed and variable capital. (Fixed capital [or assets] include all land, buildings and other facilities, durable equipment [productive or nonproductive], with the exception of items of very small unit value. Variable capital refers to materials, intermediary products, goods in process, finished products, and working capital.) Added to this are profits computed as a percentage of the gross value of assets and, thus, varying across industries.

The 1968 cost structure of major industries is shown in Table 1. A major aim of the new price system is to close the gap between consumer and producer price levels. In 1968, the difference between the two levels was quite substantial (as shown in Table 2), mainly because of 2,500 different types of turnover taxes. As a result of the reform, the number of turnover taxes was reduced to about 1,000. At the same time, more emphasis was placed on the imposition of direct taxes on enterprise operations.

Another important goal of the new price system is the establishment of individual prices that reflect cost and market conditions. To this end, the reformers developed "ideal price indexes" against which actual prices can readily be measured. Table 3 shows the deviation of actual 1968 prices from the ideal prices in several industries. Table 4 presents the same relationship for 1968 consumer products and services.

TABLE 1

Cost Structure of Hungarian Industry, 1968
(Per Cent)

Type of Cost	Industry Total
Material costs	76
Wages	13
Depreciation	4
Charge on assets and interest	6
Land rent	1
Total	100

Source: Béla Csikós-Nagy, "The New Hungarian Price System," in Reform of the Economic Mechanism in Hungary, ed. by István Friss (Budapest: Academic Publishing Co., 1969), p. 144.

TABLE 2

Producer and Consumer Price Levels, 1968
(Per Cent)

Price Level	1956	January 1, 1968
Producer	100	154
Consumer	100	104
Difference in level[a]	38	4

[a]Weighed by pattern of personal consumption.

Source: Béla Csikós-Nagy, "The New Hungarian Price System," in Reform of the Economic Mechanism in Hungary, ed. by István Friss (Budapest: Academic Publishing Co., 1969), p. 135.

TABLE 3

Deviation of Actual Prices from Ideal Prices in
Selected Industries, 1968
(Ideal Price = 100)

Branch	Ideal Price	1968 Price
Heavy industry, engineering	100	110
Light industry	100	115
Food industry	100	94
Industry total	100	106

Source: Béla Csikós-Nagy, "The New Hungarian
Price System," in Reform of the Economic Mechanism
in Hungary, ed. by István Friss (Budapest: Academic
Publishing Co., 1969), p. 137.

The reshaping of actual prices in line with
established ideal prices is a long-term project involving ten to fifteen years. In the meantime, the
reformers introduced a mixed price system made up of
(a) fixed prices applied chiefly to some basic raw
materials, important food items, and several types
of consumer goods; (b) prices subject to upper or
both upper and lower limits and applied to industrial
products, certain types of finished goods, and some
consumer products; and (c) completely free prices for
many items in all sectors of the economy.

During 1968, the first year of the reform, the
distribution of these different types of prices in
the economy was approximately as follows: In industries producing raw materials and semifinished goods,
30 per cent of the prices were fixed, 42 per cent were
subject to limitations, and 28 per cent were free; in
the finished-goods sector, 19 per cent of the prices
were fixed, 3 per cent were subject to limitations,

TABLE 4

Deviation of Actual Consumer Prices from
Ideal Prices, 1968
(Ideal Price = 100)

Products and Services	Ideal Price	1968 Price
Coal	100	55
Electric energy	100	82
Miscellaneous industrial consumer goods	100	135
Engineering products	100	118
Light industrial goods	100	132
Monopoly food products (tobacco, spirits, etc.)	100	120–50
Nonmonopoly food products (meat, milk, bakery goods, etc.)	100	70–90
Building materials	100	126
Transport and communication rates	100	74
Housing rents	100	30

Source: Béla Csikós-Nagy, "The New Hungarian
Price System" in Reform of the Economic Mechanism in
Hungary, ed. by István Friss (Budapest: Academic
Publishing Co., 1969), p. 140.

and 78 per cent were free; and, in the consumer-goods
sector, 20 per cent of the prices were fixed, 30 per
cent were subject to limitations, and 50 per cent
were free.[6]

Administration of the new price system is the
responsibility of the National Materials and Price
Office, which can call upon several economic research
institutes for information and advice.

Investment and Credit System

Pre-1968 investment decisions were made only by
the central authorities and investment funds were
free to the enterprises. In contrast, under NEM,
enterprise managers and local councils are given increased authority in making investment decisions, but
funds are no longer free.

Investments are classified in three different
categories. The first category includes major,
nationwide projects, such as the establishment of
new enterprises and the development of important
industrial branches. Decisions concerning such projects remain the responsibility of the government and
the investments are financed by the Investment Bank.
The National Planning Office includes such investments
in the medium- and long-term national plans.

The second category involves unfinished projects
that have to be completed and unprofitable ones that
may have great noneconomic significance. Decisions
concerning such investments are essentially the
responsibility of the central authorities, who may
help enterprises finance the projects out of the
state budget or through an Investment Bank loan. The
third category includes investment projects financed
by each enterprise out of its development fund. The
size of this fund is a function of the profit earned
in the market place, the ratio of the annual wage
bill to total capital assets, and an adjustment factor. The adjustment factor is designed to equalize
the substantial differences in the aforementioned
ratio among the various branches of industry. Managers have a great deal of authority to allocate the
fund among many competing uses.

The revitalized National Bank and Investment
Bank are the cornerstone of the credit system. The
National Bank grants loans to cover the variable
(working) capital needs of enterprises, whereas the
Investment Bank is limited to lending funds for fixed
capital (investment) purposes. General lending
policies are determined by the central authorities
and are defined in annual credit directives based on

the central plan objectives and general economic conditions. The credit directives specify the rate of
interest to be charged and the permissible repayment
periods for the various types of loans. They may
also include information about desirable investment
projects and activities that the banks should finance.

In granting loans, the banks have authority to
decide what type of information the applying enterprise must submit. In general, they tend to examine
the liquidity position of enterprises, profit expectations, the realism of plans, and technical as well
as managerial competence. Thus, at least theoreti-
cally, the banks have considerable influence over
enterprise managers. By granting or withholding
loans, the banks can make or break enterprises needing
investment funds or working capital.

The government is very careful not to let this
happen, however; for it wants to give enterprise
managers enough time to adjust to the new credit
system without major damage. In the long run, though,
it is quite certain that the government will take a
much less-protective attitude toward enterprise, and,
thus, the banks ultimately will become very powerful
institutions.

Employment and Labor Relations

The basis of enterprise employment policies and
labor relations is the new Labor Code passed during
1967, and implemented on January 1, 1968. The state-
ment of purpose of the new code defines its objectives
in the following manner:

> to govern participation in the work of a
> socialist society, and within this frame-
> work, specially, the rights and duties of
> enterprises and workers arising from labor
> relations, as well as the participation of
> workers through trade unions in the regu-
> lation of living and supervision of enter-
> prise activities.[7]

The new code and regulations associated with it give
enterprise managers increased authority concerning

employment, promotion, transfer, and termination
decisions. At the same time, the regulations also
enable employees to change jobs freely according to
qualifications and personal interest.

Managerial authority concerning wages and
salaries is still somewhat limited. The central
authorities determine the so-called average reference
wage, which serves as a benchmark for future wage and
salary adjustments. (In 1968, the average reference
wage represented the total 1967 wage bill of each
enterprise divided by the total number of employees.
In the same year, average wage increases were limited
to 4 per cent.)

The central authorities also develop the uni-
form occupational classification system, which includes all employees throughout industry. This
system states the qualifications, such as education
and experience, required for each occupational category and specifies the upper and lower limits of the
basic wage and salary in each category. The limits
are fixed so as to reduce to a socially and politically acceptable level the differences between basic
wages and salaries. Nevertheless, wage and salary
differences in the various occupational categories
(expressed as a percentage of the lower limit in each
case) range from about 40 per cent to 70 per cent.

The new Labor Code and associated regulations
have considerably increased the influence of labor
unions over enterprise activities. Through collective bargaining, the unions can affect wages, working
conditions, and fringe benefits. They have a voice
in the distribution of payments from the profit-
sharing fund and have to be consulted by managers
concerning employee dismissals.

Also, according to the new Labor Code, they have
the right to veto any managerial decision that "does
not meet the requirements of socialist morality" or
that breaks existing laws. Furthermore, higher
authorities, such as the branch ministries, are expected to consult the unions in appointing, promoting,
disciplining, and dismissing enterprise managers.

To prevent the misuse of this right, special
provisions were adopted. First, managerial decisions
can be vetoed only on the basis of a formal motion
accepted collectively by the local union committee.
Second, once the decision to make use of the veto
power is reached, the manager concerned has to be
immediately notified. Simultaneously, higher union
authorities have to be informed in writing about the
reasons and motives for using the veto. Only then
can higher union authorities and the representatives
of the state supervisory body, such as the branch
ministries, arbitrate the issue.

Incentive System

The acceptance of profit as the most important
enterprise success indicator resulted in the development of an incentive system that is now based on
profit. As mentioned above, a portion of enterprise
earnings is allocated to the profit-sharing fund.
(See Figure 2.) Managers may use this fund (after
the deduction of taxes and the compulsory 10-per-cent
contribution to the enterprise reserve fund) for
annual wage increases, fringe benefits, and profit-
sharing payments to employees. (Maximum average
annual wage increases are determined by the central
authorities.) Top enterprise managers and the union
plant committee jointly decide how to allocate the
money available among the three competing uses.

The distribution of profit-sharing payments--
which are made after annual wage increases and fringe-
benefits payments--is controlled by the central
authorities through a job classification scheme. In
developing it, the reformers followed two principles:
First, because every enterprise employee contributes
to the achievement of profit, each deserves a share;
and, second, because individual employee contributions are not the same, individual profit shares
should differ.

Jobs listed in the classification scheme are
divided into three categories. Top managers--such
as the general manager and his deputies, the chief
engineer, the controller, the heads of large sections,

and economic and technical consultants--are in Category I. Middle managers--such as heads of small sections and departments and technical, legal, and economic experts--belong to Category II. Finally, administrative and other supporting personnel, as well as workers, make up Category III. Within these general categories, managers have considerable authority to classify individual jobs according to the special conditions and needs of their enterprises.

The central authorities have also determined the maximum profit share that can be paid to employees in the different categories. The amount of a profit share is a percentage of the average annual salary of employees in each category. The maximum share that top managers in Category I may receive is 80 per cent; middle managers in Category II may receive 50 per cent; and employees in Category III are entitled to 15 per cent. The distribution among individuals of the total amount available in each category and the timing of such payments are left to enterprise managers. Thus, they can reward outstanding employee performance without delay and in an exceptional manner.

Individual profit shares for top managers appointed by the supervisory authorities, such as the general manager and his deputies, are determined by the same supervisory authorities. Normally, such payments represent at least the average of all profit shares paid to Category I managers. In exceptional cases, however, individual payments may exceed this average; thus, outstanding top managerial performance can also be recognized in a special way.

In addition to the profit-sharing system, employees can also be rewarded through special bonus payments. This incentive method is a carry-over from the pre-reform years, when the profit-sharing system in its present form did not exist. As of January 1, 1968, every enterprise was permitted to incorporate into its basic wage fund the same amount of money that was available for bonus payments during 1967. This amount represents the maximum that enterprise managers can use for special bonus payments under NEM.

The bonus payments are designed to serve as an incentive to employees whose contributions to enterprise operations may be of a long-range nature and, thus, cannot immediately be tied in with the annual profit earned. This does not, however, exclude those employees from also receiving profit shares in subsequent years, when their special contributions result in increased annual enterprise earnings. Enterprises and individual employees who receive official recognition in socialist labor competition can also be rewarded through bonus payments. Funds for this purpose, however, are determined and allocated by the central authorities.

Top managers can receive special bonus payments awarded by the supervisory authorities. The bonus amount, which is charged against the wage fund, may not exceed 30 per cent of the managers' basic salary. During the first few years of the reform, these payments were designed to serve not only as incentives but also as a stopgap measure. This was necessary because, before the reform, top managers received the major part of their compensation in the form of bonuses--their basic salaries were relatively low. After January 1, 1968, basic salaries were not significantly adjusted, and the reformers believed that, during the first few years of NEM, most enterprises would not make enough profit to compensate top managers through the profit-sharing fund for the loss of bonus payments. Therefore, to avoid a possible reduction of the top managers' total income, the reformers decided to continue, at least for a while, the payment of special bonuses.

If, instead of making a profit, an enterprise closes its annual operations with a financial loss, Category I and II managers are subjected to a penalty. Under such conditions, there are no profit shares to distribute and Category I managers can receive only 75 per cent of their basic annual salary; Category II managers are limited to 85 per cent of their salary. (These sanctions are even applied to managers who have, in the meantime, changed jobs. Their salary at the new place of employment has to be reduced by the appropriate amount, and the sum

involved must be transferred to the previous employer.) Category III employees, however, have to
receive their regular annual pay, without any reduc-
tions.

Foreign Trade

Hungary generates approximately 40 per cent of
its national income from foreign trade. Only three
countries in Europe--Belgium, Norway, and the Nether-
lands--obtain a higher share of national income from
their foreign-trade relations. The pre-reform trade
system in Hungary, however, was very inefficient and
rigid, and a major restructuring of that system was
considered a major objective for the long-run success
of NEM.

Under the new system, foreign-trade activities
are planned, organized, and controlled by the Minister
of Foreign Trade, who bases his decisions on the
national plan and the policy guidelines of the Economic Committee. The Minister of Foreign Trade has
authority to grant export and import licenses to
specialized foreign-trade commercial enterprises and
to industrial enterprises engaged in the production
and international marketing of their products. The
foreign exchange needed to complete international
business transactions, however, is controlled and
allocated by the National Bank.

The specialized foreign-trade commercial enterprises are authorized to represent industrial enterprises that are granted an export or import license
and to sign long-term partnership contracts with such
enterprises, sharing profit and risk. They can also
act as an agent, consignee, shipper, or marketing
representative with limited liability.

As a result of the reform, several industrial
enterprises received an import and export license
and can now independently engage in foreign-trade
activities. Import licenses were issued to enterprises that are the sole users of foreign-made products or that have formed an association for such
purpose. Export licenses were granted to enterprises

for which direct contact with a foreign trading partner is a technical necessity, to those that are the
sole producers of certain products, or to those for
which economic survival is heavily dependent on selling abroad.

Domestic and foreign market prices are linked
through foreign-exchange conversion ratios, or, as
they are officially called, foreign-trade price
multipliers. The multipliers, which represent the
average cost of exports, are based on Hungary's 1964
trade structure. They are tied in with the U.S.
dollar and the Soviet ruble. Importers and other
final users of foreign products thus pay the price
at which products were purchased in foreign markets,
converted to the domestic currency, the forint,
through the multiplier. In a similar vein, exporters
or the domestic manufacturers of products sold abroad
receive the forint equivalent of the price obtained.

As a consequence of the use of the multiplier,
the export of certain products suddenly became unprofitable, because the domestic production costs
exceeded the new, multiplier-determined price. To
prevent any serious economic dislocation in the short
run, the reformers decided to subsidize, for a period
of three years, enterprises manufacturing such products. Within this period of time, enterprise managers, however, are expected to correct the underlying
structural problems causing the high costs.

To protect the hard-currency reserves, the reformers decided to limit, somewhat, Western machine
and equipment imports that are financed through the
enterprise development fund. To this end, enterprises are required to deposit with a bank, for two
years, the forint amount of the foreign-exchange
price equivalent, multiplied by a special coefficient
determined by the central authorities. Another
import-limiting factor is the existence of quotas
for selected products and materials. These quotas
are planned at the national level and, in 1968, represented approximately 10-15 per cent of all imports.

The final limitation is the new commercial tariff
system, which is based on three different categories

of imports. The first category includes tariffs on
imports from developing countries that do not dis-
criminate against Hungarian exports and whose per
capita national income is less than that of Hungary.
The second involves tariffs on imports from socialist
and capitalist countries that have reciprocal most-
favored-nation relations with Hungary. The so-called
sanction tariffs make up the third category; these
are tariffs on imports from countries that do not
grant Hungary most-favored-nation treatment, such as
the United States.

The selling price of imported products and
materials to final users is also increased by various
import taxes and import price supplements. The former
are designed to prevent the earning of excessive
profits, whereas the latter are used as a subsidy to
importing enterprises. Both can be applied by the
Minister of Foreign Trade to all types of imports.

Enterprise Audit

The considerable decentralization of economic
decision-making authority to the enterprise level
has increased the importance of enterprise audits.
Their purpose is to evaluate the over-all economic
performance of enterprises and to determine whether
or not management has fulfilled its financial obligations toward the state. Most audits are undertaken
by the supervisory organs, such as the branch ministries or local councils. In certain cases, however,
banks, insurance companies, and specially appointed
committees can also audit enterprise operations. The
membership of such committees can vary from labor-
union to party representatives, but must always include a representative of the supervisory organs.

Every enterprise can be subjected to three
different types of audits: first, a financial audit
determining the truthfulness of enterprise balance
sheets and the correctness of tax and other payments
to the state (management has the authority to develop annual enterprise balance sheets independently
and to determine its financial obligations toward
the state); second, a supervisory audit, exercising

the ownership rights of the state, to evaluate the
over-all performance of management; and, third, an
internal audit, aimed at the safeguarding of state
property and checking for nonfinancial operating
irregularities.

Auditing teams cannot impose direct legal sanctions on management; such authority is reserved for
the Central Court of Arbitration. They can, however,
recommend to the supervisory organs the temporary
suspension of certain types of managerial decision-
making authority.

Supporting Institutions

Among other factors, the long-range success of
NEM depends upon the ability of enterprise managers
to utilize their increased economic decision-making
authority fully. Because this requires reliable and
up-to-date economic and social information on a continuous basis, the reform resulted in the revision
of the modus operandi of several existing institutions, as well as the creation of new ones.

Foremost among both the old and the new institutions collecting and processing information is the
Central Statistical Office. During the pre-reform
years, it reported chiefly on the accomplishments of
the various plan periods. Since January 1, 1968,
however, it has compiled and reported previously
rather neglected socioeconomic data useful to managers.

Magyar Hirdetö (Hungarian Advertiser), the major
promotional agency of the country, was also reorganized. Its main office is in Budapest, and its ninety
branch offices are located throughout the country.
The agency employs more than 750 people and has its
own market research department, including a public
opinion study group. Furthermore, it does its own
film and television commercials. Its services are
available to both domestic and foreign clients.

The National Market Research Agency is perhaps
one of the most important of the newly founded

informational institutions. This agency, organized
in 1967, is independent and has its own budget. Its
objectives are twofold: to develop and promote market research techniques and practices, in general,
and short-term forecasting methods, in particular;
and to perform domestic and international market
research on a contract basis. It may, at times, also
perform selected marketing functions. More than 100
people are employed by the agency. Its professional
staff is young and dynamic, and their backgrounds
range from economics to statistics.

The agency publishes Interker, which is a comprehensive monthly publication of general supply and demand conditions in domestic industrial markets. For
a reasonable fee, any enterprise may subscribe to the
publication. Another agency publication is Marketing-
Piackutatás (Marketing-Market Research), a scholarly
and management-oriented quarterly that provides
readers with information on recent domestic and international market research developments and findings.

Other relatively new institutions providing general and special economic research services and information are the Research Institute for Domestic
Trade, the Economic Research Institute, the Research
Institute for Agricultural Economics, and the Market
Research Institute attached to the Ministry of Foreign
Trade. Although, to some extent, all of these institutions compete with each other, care is taken to
minimize the duplication of efforts. The Hungarian
Chamber of Commerce also aids enterprise managers
in both the domestic and the international business
environment. It organizes meetings, lectures, and
visits for the purpose of information exchange and
publishes several periodicals in English, German,
and French, such as Marketing in Hungary.

Management Development

The Hungarian Government and economic experts
realize that implementation of the reform and its
long-range success depend chiefly on the availability
of qualified top- and middle-level managers. This
recognition of management as a critical factor in the

reform's success resulted in a fundamental change in the staffing philosophy of the central authorities.

In the past, an engineering degree almost automatically qualified its holder for a managerial position, regardless of his understanding of the concepts of modern industrial management (assuming that he was politically reliable). Technical expertise, however, is no longer enough; managers are expected to have a reasonably good understanding of the basic concepts of economics, information technology, and the behavioral sciences.

The change in the staffing philosophy of the central authorities led to corresponding changes in the education and training of managers. New institutions, such as the National Managerial Training Center, were founded to handle retraining and continuing education of the current managerial generation. To overcome the initial shortage of qualified instructors, the International Labor Organization was asked to supply staff and teaching materials. Attendance of chiefly top-level managers for differing periods of time is compulsory. Through lectures, cases, and readings, they are taught the basic concepts of finance, marketing, interpersonal relationships, and computer technology.

The branch ministries, local councils, enterprise associations, and individual enterprises themselves also organize management development seminars of various lengths. Because of the shortage of instructors and locally developed cases, the quality of these programs tends to vary considerably. Nevertheless, they provide every manager with at least an opportunity to get acquainted with modern industrial-management techniques. Education of the new managerial generation is limited to the universities and other institutions of higher learning, primarily the Karl Marx University of Economic Science in Budapest and its several off-campus schools throughout the country. No type of American or Western European business schools exists in Hungary.

The curriculum is well structured and up-to-date, although not entirely managerially oriented. The first year of study involves core courses that are required of every student. At the beginning of the second year, some specialization is possible; students can choose from among the general, commercial, and industrial areas of concentration. At the start of the third year, they can specialize even more; and, after the fourth year, they receive their final diploma, as marketing-market research, planning-analyst, or industrial-organizational specialists.

Despite the change in the staffing philosophy of the central authorities, the graduates of engineering schools and other institutions of higher learning are not disregarded as potential managers. If they perform well on the job, they can easily be promoted to middle or top managerial positions, although, prior to such promotion, they may have to participate in one of the several management development programs.

CONCLUDING REMARKS

Hungary's NEM represents a substantial move away from the complex and rigid economic system of the past. Rather, it tends toward a system of industrialization that is unique in the socialist countries of Eastern Europe. The reform does not, however, mean a return to capitalism or even to a mixed economic order of the Yugoslav type. In both its philosophy and over-all structure, NEM is firmly grounded in the tenets of Marxism-Leninism, but it is interpreted in a more flexible and pragmatic manner and according to the special economic conditions of Hungary.

The reform fundamentally changed the previously burdensome managerial environment. For the first time in over twenty years, Hungarian managers can now work without continuous interference from central bureaucrats. Managers no longer have to observe dogmatic rules and work for the attainment of utopian objectives. Most of all, the reform has substantially decreased the great disparity between managerial authority and responsibility, which was perhaps the most marked managerial characteristic of the old economic order.

This does not mean that the reform is without
its problems or that managers are no longer constrained at all. Nothing would be further from the
truth. Many expected and some unexpected problems
arose during the introductory period of the reform,
and the central authorities have not entirely given
up control over managerial decision-making. Most of
the problems, however, are the result of the essentially experimental nature of the first few years and
will probably be corrected in time. Furthermore, as
soon as the problems are corrected and a well-trained
and well-experienced managerial generation takes
over the direction of industrial enterprises, it is
very likely that the central authorities will continue
to reduce the number of managerial restrictions.

NOTES

1. Népszabadság, November 21, 1965, p. 2.

2. The discussion of the reform is based on the
following publications: Jenö Wilcsek, Vállalati
Tervezés a Gazdaságirányitás Uj Rendszerében (Enter-
prise Planning Under the New Economic Mechanism)
(Budapest: Közgazdasági és Jogi Könyvkiadó, 1967);
Lajos Ficzere, Az Állami Vállalat a Gazdaságirányitás
Uj Rendszerében (The State Enterprise Under the New
Economic Mechanism) (Budapest: Közgazdasági és Jogi
Könyvkiadó, 1970); Róbert Róka, Bankhitel a Gyakor-
latban (Bank Credit in Practice) (Budapest: Közgaz-
dasági és Jogi Könyvkiadó, 1970); István Buda and
László Pongrácz, Személyi Jövedelmek, Anyagi Érdekelt-
ség, Munka-Erö Gazdalkodás (Personal Income, Financial
Interest, Labor Economics) (Budapest: Közgazdasági
és Jogi Könyvkiadó, 1968); János Bokor, A Vállalatok
Nyereségérdekeltsége, A Vállalati Alapok (The Profit
Interest of Enterprises, Enterprise Funds) (Budapest:
Közgazdasági és Jogi Könyvkiadó, 1968); István Fürész
and Albert Katocs, A Termékfogalmazás Uj Rendje (The
New System of Distribution) (Budapest: Közgazdasági
és Jogi Könyvkiadó, 1967); Kálmán Facsády, A Vállalatok Külkereskedelmi Tevékenységének Tervezése az Uj
Gazdaságirányitás Rendszerében (The Planning of Enterprise Foreign Trade Activities Under the New Economic

Mechanism) (Budapest: Közgazdasági és Jogi Könyv-
kiadó, 1969); and István Friss, ed., Reform of the
Economic Mechanism in Hungary (Budapest: Academic
Publishing Co., 1969).

   3. Népszabadság, September 22, 1968, p. 2.

   4. Jenö Wilcsek, "The Place and Functions of
the State-Owned Enterprises in the New System of
Economic Control and Management," in Friss, ed.,
Reform of the Economic Mechanism in Hungary, p. 194.

   5. Decision of the Council of Ministers, No. 11
(May 13, 1967).

   6. Rezsö Nyers, 25 Kérdés és Válasz Gazdaság-
Politikai Kérdésekröl (25 Questions and Answers Con-
cerning Economic Policy Questions) (Budapest: Kossuth
Könyvkiadó, 1969), p. 137.

   7. Section 1, Law No. II in Magyar Közlöny
(Hungarian Gazette), October 8, 1967, p. 504.

3

At the time of NEM's introduction, the reformers considered the years 1968-70 to be the period of transition. They did not expect any immediate spectacular results, and their general attitude was one of cautious optimism. They were carefully trying to maintain the over-all balance of the economy and, unless it was unavoidable, did not want to dislocate any part of it in the short run.

As a result, the first three years of the reform were marked by a careful approach to change. Many of the previously discussed features of the reform were applied gradually and to a limited degree. Enterprise managers were given ample opportunity to adjust their operations to the new conditions without creating major upheavals in their organizations. If damage was unavoidable, the central authorities compensated for it whenever possible.

Consequently, the initial economic results of the reform, its social impact, and managerial as well as worker response to it have to be considered as only preliminary indications of possible long-range effects.[1] Although the results do provide a great deal of insight into the nature, problems, and future potential of the emerging new Hungarian economy, they do not justify a conclusive evaluation of the changes introduced on January 1, 1968.

ECONOMIC RESULTS

The report on the 1968 plan, issued by the Central Statistical Office, stated that, in general, "the achievements of the economy fulfilled the expectations better than under the old economic system."[2] During 1968, national income increased 5.1 per cent over the 1967 level, but the increase in new investments was purposely held to a low level of 1.2 per cent over those of 1967. (During 1968, the emphasis was on the completion of previously started investment projects; the number of incomplete projects was considerably less at the end of 1968 than at the beginning of the year.)

Total industrial output rose 5.3 per cent, with the chemical industry leading all other branches of the economy. Because labor productivity virtually stagnated, increasing only 1.1 per cent, industrial growth was chiefly the result of a large increase in the labor force. Worn-out machinery, lack of mechanization, the average wage control system, and the failure of management to focus on the development of labor-saving methods were given as some of the reasons for the disappointing labor-productivity results. (The change from a 48-hour to a 44-hour work week in many industries during 1968 also affected the labor-productivity developments.)

The balance of payments improved, compared to previous years; total exports increased 5 per cent, whereas imports rose only 2 per cent. More specifically, the improvement was the consequence of a 10-per-cent increase in exports to the socialist countries--above all, to the Soviet Union and Czechoslovakia. The trade balance with nonsocialist nations deteriorated to some extent, because a 2-per-cent decrease in exports to the highly developed capitalist countries and a 5-per-cent decrease in imports from them were outweighed by a negative trade relationship with the developing world.

In other areas, the performance of the economy was more promising. Both industrial producer and

consumer prices rose 1-2 per cent in 1968. This was
well within the limits set by the reformers. The
only exception was the construction industry, where
prices rose more than 4 per cent over what had been
planned, primarily because of excessive demand.

The year 1969 did not lead to any considerable
improvements over 1968, except in the foreign-trade
sector. Although national income increased 7.9 per
cent and new investments were up 7.5 per cent, total
industrial output grew only 2.9 per cent. All
branches of the economy, including the chemical industry, developed at a slower rate than during the
year before. Labor productivity continued to stagnate
(up only 0.4 per cent), because the previously mentioned structural problems could not be solved in one
year.

The balance-of-payments position improved considerably; the year ended with a 1,831 million foreign-
exchange forint surplus. Although imports from both
socialist and nonsocialist countries increased, the
favorable trade balance was the result of a 16.3-per-
cent increase in total exports. Exports to the nonsocialist countries rose a significant 32.4 per cent,
with exports of semimanufactured goods and parts
accounting for most of the increase. Per capita real
income rose 6.5 per cent, and the consumer price level
was held to a modest 1.1-per-cent increase.

The over-all performance of the economy was much
better in 1970 than during the previous two years
under NEM. True, as a consequence of serious natural
disasters, such as floods, national income increased
only 5 per cent over the previous year's figures, but
investments were up 14 per cent. Total industrial
output showed a healthy 7.4-per-cent growth; as usual,
the chemical industry, with a 15.2-per-cent increase,
was leading the field, followed by the engineering
and construction industries.

After two years of stagnation, labor productivity
finally went up 6.8 per cent, and, since the number
of people employed increased less than 1 per cent,
most of this growth could be ascribed to improved

labor performance. The balance of payments closed
with a 2,213 million foreign-exchange forint deficit,
the largest since 1957 and the result of a 30-per-
cent increase in imports of materials, machines, consumer goods, and food. (The repair of flood-caused
damages necessitated the import of many special items;
for example, the lack of meat and animal fodder necessitated the import of foods.) Per capita real
income was up another 6.5 per cent, and the consumer
price level increased only 1.1 per cent.

The Third Five-Year Plan (1966-70) ended the same
year. Over the five-year period, national income increased 31 per cent, instead of the planned 19-21 per
cent. The industrial-growth rate met the plan objectives, increasing 35 per cent over the 1965 level.
In particular, the chemical, engineering, and energy-
producing industries performed well. Labor productivity increased 61 per cent, which was well below the
planned 70-75 per cent.

During 1966-70, exports were up 53 per cent; 77
per cent of this total was made up of industrial items
and 23 per cent involved agricultural products. Imports increased 65 per cent over the 1965 level, with
the share of raw materials purchased abroad decreasing
and that of consumer goods increasing slightly. The
per capita real income of the population went up 34
per cent; the annual rate of increase in per capita
real income of industrial workers and employees
amounted to 6 per cent and that of farmers totaled
more than 7 per cent. Consequently, at the end of
the five-year period, the difference in real income
between industrial workers and farmers was significantly reduced.

GENERAL IMPACT

The introduction of NEM had been extensively
prepared by the Hungarian Government. Prior to 1968,
the basic aims of the reform and many of its details
had been widely discussed in the various mass media
and in special enterprise seminars. (Since then,
the reforms have been explained on television in a
series of animated cartoons in which important eco-

nomic concepts, such as gross national product (GNP) and productivity, have been illustrated through drawings and simple language. Another program enabled viewers to telephone in questions on the economy to Rezsö Nyers and Béla Csikós-Nagy, the two leading theoreticians of the reform.)

Under such conditions, the reform was favorably received by the population. Most Hungarian citizens recognized that, after twenty years of bureaucratic mismanagement, NEM represented a more rational approach to industrialization, which, in the long run, could probably also result in a less-restrictive political and cultural environment.

Every citizen, however, was also well aware that the reform did not signal the return of Hungary to a mixed economic system or to a Western-type political democracy. Throughout the preparatory period and after January 1, 1968, the reformers always emphasized that the party's leading role in the country's political, economic, and cultural life would not be reduced by NEM. This is recognized and accepted by the overwhelming majority of the population.

Despite the generally favorable reception, several key implications of NEM do not seem to be understood or appreciated by large segments of the population. Many people do not seem to recognize that the more rational approach to industrialization calls for a considerable increase in labor productivity and, thus, an increase in industrial discipline. This requirement, together with a continuous increase in the industrial labor force, may possibly lead to the elimination of many superfluous jobs and, thus, to some unemployment. (During 1968-70, the total industrial labor force grew at a much faster rate than during the previous years.) Although the Hungarian Government denies any such possibility, many economists admit privately that some unemployment is probably unavoidable in the long run.

An improvement of labor productivity also necessitates a realignment of basic wage and salary structures, as well as a more differentiated application

of the financial motivation system, the profit-sharing
plan. During the pre-reform years, the monthly earnings and bonuses of industrial workers frequently
surpassed the total monthly income of a professional
or a middle-level manager. Under NEM, however, contributions to the accomplishment of enterprise objectives by a professional employee, such as an
economist, or by a middle-level manager can be far
more important than is the contribution of production-
line workers.

Consequently, basic wage and salary structures
and the profit-sharing system are beginning to reflect these differences. The recognition and, most
of all, the acceptance of this fact of modern industrial life by the central authorities, however, comes
as a shock to many people, who see in these changes
a breach of socialist morality. (Through the various
mass media, the central authorities have tried to
explain that such changes are in the interest of
everybody and, thus, aid the building of socialism.)

In many cases, the reform also led to a reduction
in the number and quality of fringe benefits offered
to employees. In the past, kindergarten services,
inexpensive lunches, and free vacation facilities
were maintained by almost all enterprises. Under
NEM, enterprise management and the labor-union committee decide jointly on what type and what quality of
services employees should receive from the total fund
available for wage increases, profit-share payments,
and fringe benefits. Consequently, many of the past
services are no longer automatically offered in every
enterprise.

The reintroduction of the market place and competition into the economic system calls for a complete overhaul of existing price structures. As
pointed out in Chapter 2, the prices of many consumer products and services are still heavily subsidized. To reflect true scarcity values, the prices
of such products and services--for example, housing
and public transportation--have to be considerably increased in the long run. (The dangers associated with
a sudden increase of highly subsidized price were well

illustrated by the events in Poland during December,
1970, and January, 1971, when workers in several
industrial cities started a bloody uprising to pro-
test an increase in food prices.)

Many Hungarian citizens are uneasy about such
developments. Although they are eager to enjoy the
benefits of increased industrial efficiency under
NEM, they are not yet fully prepared to accept the
cost of a higher standard of living in terms of higher
consumer prices. Gazdaság, the quarterly of the
Hungarian Economic Association, published in 1970
some long-term (1970-85) socioeconomic and cultural
propositions of the Long-Range Hypotheses on Labor
Conditions and the Standard of Living.[3] More than
200 Hungarian professionals and intellectuals were
asked to comment on these propositions. Although
only fifty-one persons responded, their comments
clearly reflect the above-discussed concerns; the
longest and most diverging comments involved the
issues of full employment and income differentiation.

A study published by the National Market Research Agency explored the views of Hungarian citizens
on price developments after January 1, 1968.[4] Although the over-all consumer price level increased
only 1 per cent during 1968, 1.4 per cent in 1969,
and 1.3 per cent in 1970, the findings indicate that
most Hungarian citizens believe that consumer prices
are continuously increasing. Table 5 persents findings from these studies. The results concerning 1968
are quite interesting because that year was affected
by two different price developments.

As a result of a general price decrease ordered
by the central authorities, the consumer price level
during the first quarter of 1968 was 1.8 per cent
below that of March, 1967. Consequently, at the
beginning of 1968, consumers bought considerably
more butter, poultry, radio and television sets,
washing machines, and related products. Later in
the year, however, agricultural output--especially
fruits and vegetables--fell well below normal as a
result of a severe drought, and trading enterprises
did not hesitate to increase prices 15-20 per cent

TABLE 5

Consumer Opinions on Price Movements, 1969-70[a]
(Per Cent)

Prices	1969	1970
Decreased	14	8
No change	30	30
Increased	56	62

[a]Opinions concern price movements of preceding year.

   Source: "Kereskedelem-Politikai Közvéleménykutatás" (Commercial-Policy Public Poll), Marketing-Piackutatás, No. 1 (1970), p. 5.

over the 1967 level. This development was accompanied by price increases in most other consumer products, and the results of the poll probably represent consumer price-movement perceptions based on the second half of 1968.

   Table 6 shows consumer opinions concerning price movements in three major product categories. These data indicate that consumers perceived the prices of food, clothing, and durable goods as sharply increasing during the first and second years of NEM. In contrast to this, in both years, only a very few believed that the consumer price level decreased.

   Table 7 presents consumer opinions regarding the general price level in three major product categories for the year 1970 only. As can be seen, in the third year of the reform, the majority of Hungarian consumers considered prices in all three major

TABLE 6

Consumer Opinions on Price Movements in Major
Product Categories, 1969-70[a]
(Per Cent)

Prices	1969	1970
Food		
Decreased	12	5
No change	36	47
Increased	52	48
Clothing		
Decreased	14	5
No change	21	15
Increased	65	80
Durables		
Decreased	16	14
No change	32	28
Increased	52	58

[a]Opinions concern price movements of preceding
year.

   Source: "Kereskedelem-Politikai Közvéleménykutatás" (Commercial-Policy Public Poll), Marketing-
Piackutatás, No. 1 (1970), p. 5.

product categories to be very high or a little too
high. Within the different categories, they singled
out meat, men's and women's outerwear, shoes, and
kitchen equipment as the highest-priced items.

   It is interesting to note that most consumers
tended to believe that prices were continuously going
up because industrial and commercial enterprises were
eager to increase their profit. The partial validity
of this argument notwithstanding, however, not too
many consumers recognized that some of the price increases were the result of the slow and gradual adjustment of the over-all price level to the market
realities of NEM.

TABLE 7

Consumer Opinions on General Price Levels in
Major Product Categories, 1970
(Per Cent)

Prices	Food	Clothing	Durables
Very high	17	31	20
Little too high	35	47	39
Acceptable	48	22	41
Low	0	0	0

Source: "Kereskedelem-Politikai Közvéleménykutatás (Commercial-Policy Public Poll), Marketing-
Piackutatás, No. 1 (1970), p. 6.

The National Market Research Agency studies also
found that many Hungarian consumers were dissatisfied
with the product assortment offered for sale during
1970; Table 8 summarizes consumer opinions on this
subject. These data show that, with respect to food
and clothing, consumers tended to be most dissatisfied
with the price choices offered and also complained
about the unavailability of certain food items, such
as good meat. Durable goods seemed to be in serious
shortage, inasmuch as 64 per cent of those interviewed
indicated that, in most cases, they did not find the
product that they were looking for.

The over-all results of this study are quite
informative. They do, to some extent, reflect the
high expectations of most Hungarians concerning the
immediate results of the reform. It seems that consumers expected all industrial and commercial enterprises to start producing a wide assortment of

TABLE 8

Reasons for Consumer Dissatisfaction with Product
Assortment, 1970
(Per Cent)

Reasons	Major Product Categories		
	Food	Clothing	Durables
Lack of price choice	27	28	5
Lack of size choice	0	8	0
Lack of fashion choice	0	2	0
Lack of availability	38	14	64
Lack of desired quality	18	12	1
Lack of spare parts	0	0	23
Lack of proper sales timing	5	4	2

Source: "Kereskedelem-Politikai Közvéleménykutatás (Commercial-Policy Public Poll), Marketing-Piackutatás, No. 1 (1970), p. 8.

reasonably priced and good-quality products immediately. Most Hungarians are sophisticated consumers; they are price, quality, and style conscious and thus show little patience for the initial trial-and-error production and marketing policies of most industrial and commercial enterprises.

The central authorities anticipated the initial difficulties, and, to overcome the lack of a satisfactory product assortment, at least partially, they increased the importation of many kinds of consumer goods from both the socialist and nonsocialist countries in 1968. (Another objective of such imports was to stimulate competition in the domestic market place.) Consequently, retail shops in Budapest and other major cities are quite well stocked with

Italian shoes and clothing items, Scotch whiskey,
French cognac and perfume, and American cigarettes
and cosmetics. True, as a result of foreign-exchange
limitations and the use of the foreign-trade price
multiplier, most of these products are very highly
priced and, thus, out of reach for many Hungarians.
But, after many years marked by their total absence,
such products are at least available to those who
can afford them.

Despite the continuous price increases perceived
by most Hungarian consumers since 1968, per capita
real income went up during the first three years of
the reform. During 1968, it increased 5.5 per cent;
in 1969, 6.5 per cent; and in 1970, 6.5 per cent.[5]
As a consequence of productivity increases and, most
of all, as a result of an increase in food prices,
the per capita real income of farmers improved significantly during 1968-70.

The structure of income distribution has also
changed. Table 9 summarizes the distribution of per
capita monthly income for the total population in
1965 and 1970. These data show that the percentage
of people falling into the lowest category (less than
600 forint per month) has decreased, whereas the
percentage of people in the highest category (over
2,000 forint per month) has considerably increased.
(In both 1965 and 1970, the majority of the population
fell into the 800-1,600 forint category. Their proportion, however, was 55 per cent in 1970, as opposed
to 53 per cent in 1965.) It is important to point
out that most of these changes took place during the
first three years of the reform.

The increase in per capita real income and the
improvements in the structure of income distribution
have also affected savings patterns. During 1961-67,
total savings, relative to the net monetary income
of the population, grew by an annual average of 2.7
per cent; since 1968, however, they have increased
at a considerably faster rate. Table 10 summarizes
these developments. The increase in the propensity
to save during the first three years of the reform
was also affected by the unavailability of many

TABLE 9

Per Capita Distribution of Monthly Income,
1965 and 1970
(Per Cent)

Income (forint)[a]	1965	1970
Less than 600	17.7	4.9
600-800	20.2	9.1
800-1,000	19.9	13.5
1,000-1,200	15.6	15.3
1,200-1,400	10.6	14.4
1,400-1,600	6.7	12.1
1,600-1,800	4.0	9.4
1,800-2,000	2.3	6.9
More than 2,000	3.0	14.4

[a]At official exchange rate of 30 forint to U.S. $1.

Source: Figyelö, May 23, 1971, p. 3.

TABLE 10

Increase in Total Savings Relative to Net Monetary
Income, 1968-70
(Per Cent)

Year	Rate of Increase
1968	3.2
1969	4.0
1970	5.0

Source: Statisztikai Évkönyv 1969 (Statistical
Yearbook 1969) (Budapest: Központi Statisztikai
Hivatal, 1970), p. 238.

durable goods that consumers wanted to buy. Consequently, as soon as some of these items, such as
cars, are available in adequate numbers to satisfy
demand, a substantial part of these saving deposits
may immediately be withdrawn.

MANAGERIAL IMPACT

The effects of NEM on managers during 1968-70
were rather severe. The change from a command,
planned economy to a relatively free and increasingly
competitive, market-oriented one initially resulted
in shock, apprehension, and confusion on the part of
the managers. It resulted in shock because many managers were psychologically and professionally not ready
to deal with the changes introduced under NEM and,
thus, to perform their duties effectively in the new
environment. Although the central authorities had
tried to prepare managers for the reform since 1965,
the preparations consisted chiefly of the formal
dissemination of information. Thus, although most
managers probably understood the formal aspects of
NEM, their mental habits and behavioral traits, shaped
over a period of twenty years, remained largely un-
affected.

Consequently, at first, many managers had difficulties adjusting to the new environment. Through
centrally administered development programs, self-
education, and trial-and-error experience on the job,
however, more and more managers began to understand
and to appreciate their new role. This was not an
easy process, because managers not only had to start
changing their own attitudes and behavior but also
had to restructure their own organizations fundamentally and re-educate the employees. They had to
introduce subordinates to the implications of NEM at
both the macro and the enterprise level and explain
the new motivational system and the role of profit,
as well as competition.

They were also expected to promote the use of
new problem-solving techniques and, naturally, to
perform the routine tasks involved in the day-to-day

management of enterprise operations. The natural talents and goodwill of many managers notwithstanding, it is understandable that, initially, most of them were shocked by the dual demands of their new role under NEM as activist-catalyst change agents. Although most managers seem to have overcome the initial difficulties of adjustment, many attitude and behavior problems remain unsolved. (These will be discussed in Chapter 4.)

The reform resulted in apprehension because numerous managers were afraid of losing their comfortable and well-paying jobs, which, in the past, they may have received as a reward for long and dedicated party membership or special technical expertise, such as engineering experience. As pointed out in Chapter 2, already during the early 1960's, the central authorities considered both political reliability and technical expertise to be key managerial selection standards. Therefore, during those years, some politically reliable, but technically incompetent, managers had to accept transfers to less-important positions or quietly retire.

Under NEM, the issue of managerial selection became important again, albeit in a somewhat more-complex form. Since January 1, 1968, managers have been selected on the basis of political reliability, technical expertise, and administrative ability.[6] Consequently, political reliability and technical expertise alone, or even together, are no longer enough to assure a manager who lacks administrative ability of his position on a continuous basis. Furthermore, the central authorities weighed all three standards equally, and, thus, many managers appointed during the pre-reform years felt very insecure.

This managerial insecurity and the resulting apprehension were not entirely justified. The central authorities did not immediately discharge or transfer all managers who did not meet the new requirements. As a matter of policy, they removed only those who were totally incompetent and gave all the others an opportunity to prove themselves under NEM. New managerial appointments, however, were essentially limited to those individuals who met all three requirements in a reasonably satisfactory manner.

This new staffing policy, nevertheless, did not go unnoticed and created some ill feelings, especially among the party faithful. Already in 1967, for example, the party newspaper, Pártélet (Party Life), argued that

> in filling central administrative and enterprise jobs in a one-sided manner, skill is the determining factor and political requirements are neglected . . . Central administrative and enterprise leaders, exaggerating the need for training, do not like to admit party members to their domain. Recently, some experts, who were not entirely politically reliable, received appointments to leading positions.[7]

Although the central authorities did not condone such developments and thus tried to prevent their occurrence whenever possible, they also continued to insist that political reliability could never again become the most important managerial selection standard.[8]

The introduction of NEM also created some confusion among managers. This was partially the result of the shock and apprehension described above and partially because of the initial errors and misunderstandings accompanying such a large-scale reorganization of the economy and the industrial authority structure. Despite the careful preparation of the reform, many directives were initially misinterpreted and misapplied by both the central authorities and the managers.

Uncertainty as to the precise meaning of the new rules and their effects on enterprise employees and operations was widespread. Many managers had to feel their way through trial-and-error processes and had to display a great deal of understanding and patience for their employees, who experienced similar problems. It is necessary to point out, however, that in no enterprise did this initial confusion lead to serious operational breakdowns.

The acceptance by the central authorities of management as a critical factor in the long-range success of NEM led to a widespread social recognition of managers as an important and influential group. The most tangible part of this recognition was an increase in their total income. Although basic managerial salaries were not increased to any significant degree, managers were more than compensated for this through the extra income that they received from the profit-sharing plan and special bonus payments.

Table 11 presents the relationship between the total income of managers, workers, and supporting personnel during the first two years of the reform. It is clear from this summary presentation that both top- and middle-level managers could improve their standard of living substantially relative to workers and supporting personnel. By the end of 1970, most top managers already owned private cars, weekend

TABLE 11

Relationship Between Total Income of Managers, Workers, and Supporting Personnel, 1968-69[a]

Position	1968	1969
Top managers	2.65	2.94
Middle managers	1.71	1.83
Workers and supporting personnel	1.00	1.00

[a]Total income of workers and supporting personnel equals 1.

Source: Figyelö, May 26, 1971, p. 3.

homes, or a piece of property along the shores of
the fashionable Lake Balaton.

Middle managers, although their total earnings
were less than those of top managers, have also
changed their style of life. By the end of 1970,
and, certainly, by 1971, many of them had also bought
private cars or weekend homes, albeit perhaps of a
somewhat less-expensive type than the ones purchased
by top managers. Consequently, soon after the implementation of NEM, it became apparent that managers
as a group started to emerge as a new, technocratic
elite of Hungarian society.

Although the central authorities recognized the
inherent dangers of such developments, they also
acknowledged that, under NEM, income differentiation
between managers and other employees was necessary
and unavoidable. Critics of these managerial incomes
were told by the central authorities that

> they fail to see that income according to
> work involves both equality and inequality.
> It involves equality because exploitation
> has disappeared; work is the only way to
> obtain the income every citizen is entitled
> to . . . Egalitarianism, however, would
> understandably discourage all those whose
> hard work, knowledge, and skill offer
> society more and better things . . . Now-
> days it is more justified than before that
> importance and responsibility of work should
> be reflected in income differences.[9]

During the first two years of the reform, such arguments were not too well received by most Hungarians.
Many workers and supporting employees believed that
such a high degree of income differentiation was
incompatible with socialist morality and that, therefore, managerial incomes should be reduced. By the
end of 1970, however, as a result of subsequent
changes in the profit-sharing system and the passage
of time, the idea of a highly differentiated income
structure favoring managers over all other groups

tended to be accepted by most Hungarian citizens.
(The subsequent changes will be discussed in Chapters
4 and 5.)

WORKER IMPACT

The initial effect of NEM on industrial workers
was, in many ways, similar to that on managers. Despite the earnest efforts of the central authorities
and managers to explain the major features of the
new system and reasons for it, many industrial workers
had difficulties grasping and interpreting the essence
of the changes. As in the case of any change situation, the problems were compounded by the tendency
of informal enterprise communication channels to disseminate half-truths concerning the new industrial
working conditions, pay and norm adjustments, and
the new financial motivation system.

Influenced by such rumors, some workers looked
upon the reform as a panacea for all their problems;
others believed that it would make life more difficult. The initial confusion--which was caused by
the reorganization of internal enterprise operations
and by the authoritarian behavior, errors, and,
occasionally, resentful attitudes of some managers--
increased the apprehensive feeling that many workers
had at this time.

As pointed out previously, workers resented most
of all the new profit-sharing system, according to
which they were placed in Category III and, thus,
could receive, at a maximum, only 15 per cent of
their annual average salary for good work performance.
(See the discussion under "Incentive System," in
Chapter 2.) Consequently, many workers considered
the new arrangements unfair.[10] In particular, those
workers who, in the past, could easily have earned
more than middle-level or even top-level managers
were irked, even though the maximum 15-per-cent
profit share meant almost twice as much in monetary
terms as the amount they could receive under the pre-
reform bonus system.

The average annual real income of industrial
workers increased 6.3 per cent during 1968-70.
Table 12 presents a breakdown of this increase on
a yearly basis and compares it with the increases
in real income of agricultural workers. Although
the average annual real income increase of agricultural workers during 1968-70 was somewhat higher
(7.0 per cent) than that of industrial workers, this
increase helped only to reduce the long-standing income gap between the two groups. By the end of 1970,
industrial workers were still better off than were
agricultural workers.

The reduction in the average work week from 48
hours to 44 hours in many industries during 1968-70
provided additional sources of income for industrial
workers. To keep their enterprises running, many
managers authorized overtime, and the possibilities
for moonlighting in second jobs were excellent.
Skilled workers--for example, plumbers, electricians,
car mechanics, and masons--had no difficulty earning
extra income. Second jobs became so widespread that

TABLE 12

Comparison of Annual Real Income Increases of
Industrial and Agricultural Workers, 1968-70
(Previous Year = 100)

Year	Industrial Workers	Agricultural Workers
1968	106	108
1969	106	105
1970	107	108

Source: Statisztikai Évkönyv 1969 (Statistical
Yearbook 1969) (Budapest: Központi Statisztikai
Hivatal, 1970), p. 228.

some managers charged that many skilled industrial
workers seemed to rest at their place of full employment in order to be in good shape for the weekend
when they were moonlighting.

The new Labor Code governing industrial relations
was well received by most workers. A more active
union, independent collective bargaining, some veto
power over managerial decisions, and the freedom to
change jobs according to personal needs and desires
represented a giant step in the direction of better
and more satisfying working conditions. This was
so, even though, during the first three years of the
reform, many union leaders and enterprise industrial-
relations experts were not quite sure how to engage
in fruitful collective bargaining.

A study by the Ministry of Labor involving collective-bargaining experience in sixty-one enterprises during 1968 and 1969, for example, showed that
most agreements lacked a sound economic basis.[11]
Wage and income-policy guidelines were omitted, the
financial aspects of the motivational system were
neglected, and other contract stipulations were developed in an ad hoc manner. At the same time, the
study reported, many collective agreements seriously
limited the disciplinary authority of enterprise
managers. This seemed to indicate that, in exercising
their newly won power, union leaders were taking full
advantage of the industrial labor shortage and the
resulting managerial concern about dissatisfied workers quitting their jobs.

Although the total industrial labor force grew
2.2 per cent in 1968 and 1.6 per cent in 1969, most
industrial enterprises were plagued by a persistent
labor shortage during the first three years of NEM.
This shortage, together with the freedom to choose
jobs, resulted in a very high rate of labor mobility.
In 1968, out of 3.6 million employees in the state-
owned sector of the economy, 1.5 million changed
jobs.[12] In 1969, this number increased to 1.6 million, and approximately 500,000 of these workers
changed their jobs several times. The managers of
industrial enterprises in Budapest, for example, in

order to add 100 permanent employees to their work force in 1969, had to hire 6,300 workers throughout the year.[13]

Some of this mobility was desirable and necessary in order to reallocate the labor force from stagnating industries to growing ones. Most individual workers who changed jobs, however, looked for higher pay, improved working conditions, better advancement opportunities, or a plant closer to home. These features were not always offered only by the growth industries, and, thus, a large part of this high degree of labor mobility was not beneficial from the point of view of the economy as a whole.

CONCLUDING REMARKS

Despite the expected difficulties of transformation, the initial results of NEM seemed promising. After two years of rather uncertain performance, the economy as a whole justified the modest, but confident, expectations of the reformers in 1970. Although many Hungarian citizens did not seem to understand the long-range implications of NEM fully and thus complained about the implications of some of the changes (for example, price increases), the overwhelming majority welcomed the increase in the standard of living and the general relaxation of the formerly burdensome economic and industrial rules and regulations.

Industrial managers as a group have greatly benefited from NEM. After an initial period of shock and some apprehension, the able managers seemed to have emerged, by the end of 1970, as the new technocratic elite of Hungarian society. Well treated by the central authorities and respected (as well as envied) by many Hungarians, they have started to enjoy both the tangible and the intangible rewards of their new role.

Workers appeared to react in a similar manner. Initially, they were somewhat suspicious and did not fully understand all the implications of NEM. By the

end of 1970, however, together with a noticeable
improvement in their standard of living, they seemed
to have more confidence in both the central authorities and the long-range success of NEM.

NOTES

    1. Economic results are based on Statisztikai
Évkönyv 1969 (Statistical Yearbook 1969) (Budapest:
Központi Statisztikai Hivatal, 1970).

    2. Népszabadság, February 2, 1969, p. 2.

    3. Zsuzsa Ferge and Kálmán Rupp, "A Munkaerö
és Életszínvonal Távlati Tervezési Hipotéziseinek
Vitája" (The Discussion Concerning the Long-Range
Hypotheses on Labor Conditions and the Standard of
Living), Gazdaság, December, 1970, pp. 61-72.

    4. "Kereskedelem-Politikai Közvéleménykutatás"
(Commercial-Policy Public Poll), Marketing-Piackutatás,
No. 1 (1970); p. 5.

    5. Statisztikai Évkönyv 1969 (Statistical Year-
book 1969), p. 36.

    6. Rezsö Nyers, 25 Kérdés és Válasz Gazdaság-
Politikai Kérdésekröl (25 Questions and Answers Con-
cerning Economic Policy Questions) (Budapest: Kossuth
Könyvkiadó, 1969), p. 53.

    7. Pártélet (Party Life), October, 1967, p. 2.

    8. Nyers, 25 Kérdés és Válasz (25 Questions and
Answers), p. 53.

    9. Népszabadság, January 26, 1968, p. 3.

    10. Ibid., January 9, 1968, p. 2.

    11. Figyelö, January 13, 1971, p. 1.

    12. Ibid., January 21, 1970, p. 1.

    13. Ibid.

4

A fundamental reorganization of any economic system is bound to create a multitude of technical and human problems. The Hungarian NEM is no exception. During the first three years of its existence, NEM generated many problems for both the central authorities and the enterprise managers.

From a managerial viewpoint, some of the problems during 1968-70 were of a general and uncontrollable nature; they were generated by the structural characteristics of the Hungarian economy and by past and current politico-economic decisions of the central authorities. Other problems were of a more special, operational nature and were caused partially by certain features of NEM and partially by certain managerial attitudes and behavior. Such problems were, to some extent, subject to corrective managerial influence. Finally, some problems were caused chiefly, if not entirely, by managerial attitudes and behavior and, thus, could be corrected only by the managers themselves.

The existence of problems in itself does not determine the long-range prospects of a new economic and managerial system; rather, it is the nature and effectiveness of proposed corrective actions that are important in this situation. Consequently, the 1968-70 problems of NEM should not be interpreted as

inherent and permanent weaknesses. For long-range
evaluation purposes, the problems should be interpreted in light of the various adjustments and developments that took place during 1970 or those that are
planned for the 1971-75 period. (The 1970 changes
and adjustments will be discussed here; the 1971-75
changes and adjustments will be treated in Chapter 5.)

GENERAL PROBLEMS

The more-general problems were generated chiefly
by the structure of the Hungarian economy and by
past, as well as current, politico-economic decisions
of the central authorities. These problems strongly
affected the performance of managerial functions at
the enterprise level and were, from a managerial
viewpoint, uncontrollable.

Limited Theoretical Foundation

For several years prior to January 1, 1968, the
Hungarian central authorities and academic community
worked to develop the theoretical foundations of
NEM. The magnitude of the change-over and the ideological implications of the reform, however, made it
impossible for them to complete the theoretical foundations on time. Although many books, articles,
studies, and pamphlets had been published on NEM,
most of this literature dealt chiefly with the administrative aspects of the reform. The difficulty of
completing the comprehensive reform was understandable, because, apart from Yugoslavia, no other socialist country had embarked on such a large-scale
and ambitious project as NEM. Consequently, the
Hungarian reformers had few, if any, theoretical and
empirical guidelines to follow.

Traditional Marxian economics, although they
formed the ideological basis of the reform, could
not provide the needed theoretical concepts, because
they do not deal with such key issues of NEM as profit, rate of interest, competition, and the market
place.[1] Furthermore, traditional Marxian economics,

unlike modern capitalist economic theory, are not
complemented by the discipline of business administration and, thus, lack the large body of empirically
tested, managerial decision-making guidelines necessary for the development of a decentralized and competitively oriented socialist economic system.

Consequently, the reformers had to adopt and
try to modify many concepts of modern capitalist economic theory and business administration. This process was not an easy one, because the new concepts
had to be not only operationally useful but also
ideologically acceptable. As could be expected, the
adaptation of capitalist concepts resulted in many
heated debates and arguments.

To illustrate the point, marketing, which in
the past was almost entirely ignored in Hungary, became a very important enterprise function under NEM.
As a result of the industrial managers' almost total
lack of understanding of modern marketing methods
and the virtual absence of domestic literature on
the subject, the Hungarian reformers had to turn to
Western, especially American, publications for marketing information. This, naturally, led to debates
concerning the necessity of a socialist interpretation of the marketing function and the applicability
of capitalist marketing methods in a socialist economy.[2]

The debaters pointed out, for example, that, in
a socialist economy, the market place performs essentially the same functions as in a capitalist economy,
but under entirely different conditions, because not
only does the socialist market place regulate the allocation of goods and services but it is itself
highly regulated by the central authorities.[3] In regard to the applicability of capitalist marketing
methods, all Hungarian discussants agreed that there
are fundamental political and economic differences
between the two economic systems. Thus, the marketing methods developed and utilized in capitalist
economies cannot be used in socialist economies without modification.

Although one of the debaters argued that marketing is essentially the application of scientific
methodology and, thus, is as free of "class influences" as is mathematics, the general consensus was
that too many major differences existed between the
two systems to accept such an argument without any
reservations. The major differences were said to
be the varying magnitudes and characteristics of the
market places, the fundamentally different competitive conditions, and differences in the availability
of advanced information-processing equipment.[4] This
discussant also emphasized that socialist economies
can shape and formulate marketing activities at the
macro level, whereas capitalist systems can utilize
marketing only at the micro, or firm, level.

Most of the criticism was directed against advertising and public relations. The debaters emphasized that, in capitalist economies, advertising
and public relations tend to promote excessive competition and thus help amplify the anarchistic conditions in the market place. In socialist economies,
the discussants continued, advertising and public
relations are utilized in a well-regulated market
and in a planned fashion; thus, they tend to aid in
the development of the socialist economies.

One Hungarian debater also questioned the applicability of capitalist market research methods. He
argued that formal methods, such as statistics,
could be used, but emphasized that the essence of
market research is not the collection of data, but
its interpretation.[5] Such interpretation, however,
is a function of the socioeconomic conditions under
which it takes place. Thus, he emphasized, the
methods used to interpret data collected through
similar statistical techniques have to be different
in socialist, as opposed to capitalist economies.

Discussions, such as the marketing debate, were
necessary and unavoidable. Because they were usually
of a theoretical nature and did not provide industrial
managers with decision-making guides, they tended to
be unproductive in the short run. Therefore, at the
enterprise level, many aspects of NEM had to be

implemented on a trial-and-error basis. This was a costly procedure because it quite often led to mis-interpretations and, thus, to confusion and uncertainty among managers and workers. It was in this fashion that the lack of a solid theoretical foundation in many areas of NEM created problems for managers in their daily operations.

Lack of Satisfactory Planning
Information

As pointed out in Chapter 2, the Hungarian economy under NEM continues to be centrally planned: major economic, social, and cultural objectives are defined in official fifteen- and five-year plans. The economy in general and individual enterprises in particular are influenced toward desired plan objectives through the selective use of economic regulators, such as taxation, credit policies, and foreign-exchange allocations. Managers are also strongly advised by the central authorities to use the central plan and associated information as basic premises in the development of enterprise plans.

The experiences of the first three reform years, however, indicate that most enterprise managers were not satisfied with the quality of planning information disseminated by the central authorities. A study by the Industrial Research Group of the Hungarian Academy of Sciences, for example, found that 54 per cent of the industrial managers polled believed that official information concerning industry developments was not satisfactory.[6] Furthermore, 62 per cent argued that over-all economic information was not good enough, and 66 per cent complained that information about the economic regulators did not meet their expectations. Finally, 74 per cent of the managers were critical of information dealing with the economic policy conceptions of the central authorities.

Most of the criticism expressed by the managers was justified. Medium- and long-term policy conceptions were not always spelled out clearly by the central authorities, and information concerning the economic regulators was occasionally limited. This

made enterprise planning a difficult task and impeded
the development of a good relationship between central and enterprise plans. Occasionally, however,
criticism by the managers was only a means of cover-
ing up their own inabilities to deal with uncertainty
and risk. (In the Hungarian Academy of Sciences
study, for example, four enterprises whose managers
complained about the quality of industry information
available were in a monopoly position.) These managers apparently expected the central authorities to
supply information that would eliminate uncertainty,
as well as minimize risk, which, of course, would
have undermined one of the essential competitive elements of NEM.

Lack of Competition

As discussed in Chapter 2, NEM was expected to
reintroduce competition into the market place gradually and, thus, eventually to increase the over-all
efficiency of Hungarian industry. The reformers
recognized, however, that, for many industries, competition had to be severely limited, because a sudden exposure to market forces could easily have led
to these industries' elimination. For political,
economic, and social reasons, such an outcome would
have been unacceptable, and, thus, the protective
attitude of the central authorities during most of
1968-70 was understandable.

It soon became apparent, however, that the development of competitive conditions was behind the
planned schedule and that most markets were still
dominated by large enterprises enjoying quasi- or
full-monopoly positions. These large enterprises
were not the result of economies of scale in production, but of the administrative reorganizational
decisions of the central authorities during the pre-
reform years. By virtue of their size and market
position, they severely limited competition.

A 1968 study, for example, found that 38 per
cent of the industrial enterprises sampled had no
domestic competition, 46 per cent had no import competition, and 21 per cent had neither type.[7]

absence of modern small and medium-sized industrial
enterprises in the Hungarian economy not only limited
competition but, also, was partially responsible for
the limited product choice in many markets. Most
large enterprises did not find it economical to manufacture certain products, and, since there were no
small or medium-sized enterprises to fill the void,
demand for such products could not be satisfied.

Even before 1968, the central authorities recognized that the problem of competition would be a
crucial one. Initially, they believed that competition in most markets could be increased through more
imports and eventual capital movements from industry
to industry and that product choice could be improved.
The experiences of the first three years, however,
indicated that the other socialist countries were
not able to provide the needed product assortment and
that imports from the more flexible nonsocialist markets were limited by hard-currency shortages. In addition, the expected capital movements did not take
place. Most managers were very conservative risk-
takers and thus refrained from entering new markets
or forming new enterprise associations. They seemed
to be quite content with the relatively safe market
position that their enterprises enjoyed. Therefore,
in April, 1970, the cabinet-level Economic Committee
instructed the heads of all national economic agencies, such as the branch ministries, to develop plans
and methods for the creation of small and medium-
sized industrial enterprises in their respective
branches. In its instructions, the committee also
outlined the methods of financing such new enterprises and emphasized the need for immediate action.

The lack of competition in many markets not only
affected the efficient over-all allocation of resources and the available product choice in terms of
type, quality, and price but also negatively influenced managerial attitudes and behavior. Not forced
by competition to improve internal enterprise operations immediately, many industrial managers were slow
to identify sources of organizational inefficiency,
to tighten work discipline, and to adopt modern management techniques.

Limited Role of Profit

The reintroduction of the market place and competition resulted in, among other factors, the acceptance of profit as the most important enterprise
success indicator. The lack of competition and the
resulting seller's market, however, considerably
limited the usefulness of profit as an indicator of
enterprise performance. During the first three years
of the reform, the high rate of profit earned by many
enterprises was not the result of increased production efficiency or of better marketing but of the
quasi- or full-monopoly positions that they enjoyed
in the market place.

Direct and indirect subsidies to various industrial enterprises also limited the success indicator
role of profit. Although, during the transitional
period, most subsidies could be justified on political and social grounds, the rate of increase in total
funds granted during the first three years was stag-
gering. (Indirect subsidies consisted chiefly of
tax concessions, preferential interest rates, and
better credit terms.) According to official figures,
between 1967 and 1971 the amount of direct subsidies
increased from 36 billion to 57 billion forint or,
in other words, to almost one-fifth of national income.[8] Almost one-third of this amount was granted
to enterprises that needed support to maintain unprofitable, but politically and socially desirable,
activities. The rest of the subsidies were used to
promote the competitiveness of export industries and
to relate the domestic prices of imported products
to world market prices.

The generous subsidy policies of the central
authorities negatively affected the efficient allocation of resources in the Hungarian economy. In
addition, they reintroduced the idea of bargaining
between the central authorities and the enterprise
managers. In pre-reform years, the centrally developed enterprise plan and the counterplan worked out
by the managers provided the basis for protracted
bargaining. During the first three years of NEM,
the willingness of the central authorities to support

some inefficient and, thus, probably badly managed
enterprises created similar situations.

Already, at the start of the reform, many managers argued that, as a result of special conditions,
their organizations were at a disadvantage relative
to other enterprises. Therefore, they claimed, their
enterprises were entitled to subsidies. The central
authorities, to minimize the dislocations of the
transitional period, were receptive to such arguments;
however, since they lacked a set of well-defined standards to evaluate the subsidy requests in an economical fashion, many nondeserving enterprises received
substantial amounts of direct and indirect aid.

Many such nondeserving enterprises not only sur-
vived but, as a result of the subsidies, also showed
a good profit and thus generated a development fund.
This fund, as explained in Chapter 2, could be used
by management for investment purposes, and, therefore,
several inefficient enterprises, instead of curtail-
ing their operations, actually expanded. Like the
lack of competition, the limited success indicator
role of profit tended to affect managerial attitudes
and behavior negatively. Protected against the direct
consequences of inefficient operations, many industrial managers could continue to postpone long-overdue
internal reorganizations, revisions of product lines,
and critical investigations of other enterprise activities.

Shortage of Qualified Managers
and Specialists

The shortage of qualified managers at every organizational level was a major problem under NEM.
The reformers recognized that the long-range success
of NEM depended on the availability of well-trained
managers, and, consequently, all top enterprise managers were required to attend development programs
regularly at the National Managerial Training Center.
Because of the lack of facilities and instructors and
the pressure of time, however, most middle managers
could not be included in these programs. This was
very unfortunate, because, for the most part, these

managers were not qualified to provide top managers
with needed support. Most middle managers tended to
act only as mechanical executors of top managerial
directives, and such timid and unimaginative behavior,
in turn, seemed to convince top managers that they
were justified in not delegating more decision-making
authority to middle managers. As a consequence, most
industrial enterprises were overcentralized and were
organized in a far more complex fashion than was necessary.

The shortage of well-qualified middle managers
was further compounded by the shortage of well-trained
staff specialists, who were needed to advise both
top and middle managers in their daily activities.
Specialists in data-processing, information systems,
and market research were especially in short supply.
By the end of 1970, for example, there were 120 com-
puters in Hungary, but only about 2,000 trained computer specialists, such as programmers, technicians,
and other service personnel.[9]

In an attempt to overcome this problem, computer installations employed high school mathematics
teachers, but, unfortunately, not too many were know-
ledgeable about computer applications. Because experienced market researchers were also rare, many enterprises had considerable difficulty organizing
their market research departments and thus had to employ outside consultants. But even well-qualified
outside consultants were difficult to find, and managers frequently had to make important decisions without expert advice.

Under such conditions, most industrial enterprises, although having reasonably well-trained top
managers, were not staffed with an adequate number
of equally well-trained middle managers and staff
specialists. When top managers returned from the
various development programs, they frequently found
it very difficult to disseminate the newly acquired
knowledge among their subordinates. Many innovative
ideas were not understood by the middle managers and
were thus misinterpreted and misapplied.

In addition to causing short-term operational
problems, the shortage of well-qualified middle managers had serious long-range implications, because
vacant top managerial positions had to be filled
chiefly from the ranks of middle managers. As the
Hungarian economy continues to expand, the demand
for qualified top managers will also increase more
and more, and the shortage of well-trained middle
managers could easily reach critical proportions
within a few years.

PROBLEMS OF MANAGERIAL ENVIRONMENT

In addition to the managerially uncontrollable
problems, managers also had to deal with difficulties
generated by the new environment. Problems in this
category were of a special, operational nature. They
were caused partially by various decisions of the central authorities concerning the major features of
NEM and partially by managerial attitudes and behavior.

Managerial Independence

An essential feature of NEM was the large-scale
decentralization of economic decision-making authority
to the enterprise level. As discussed in Chapter 3,
this resulted in a new industrial authority structure
that considerably simplified the relationship between
the supervisory branch ministries and the enterprise
managers. Although the reformers outlined the general
nature of this relationship, they recognized that it
was impossible to foresee every possible turn of
events and, therefore, assumed that the specific details would be worked out by the branch ministries
and managers in a mutually satisfactory manner.

Some reformers and observers expected that the
branch ministries would be reluctant to give up the
authority that they possessed during the pre-reform
years.[10] True, for a while, some old-line bureaucrats attempted to reestablish ministry control over
many enterprise activities. This created misunderstandings, but, interestingly, most of the managerial

independence problems were created by the managers
themselves, who were extremely jealous of their newly
won authority and frequently attacked the branch ministries, without justification, for "bureaucratic
interference" in their activities.

This negative managerial attitude toward the
branch ministries was noticed even by the political
leadership. To strengthen the authority of the supervisory ministries, the report of the Central Committee
at the Tenth Party Congress stated the following:
"We must also overcome the uncertain, waiting attitude of some state organs and ministries who, as if
time stood still, do not want to issue directives
[to enterprises] even after the problems are identified and action is called for."[11]

Managerial independence was also a problem in
the relationship between management and enterprise
party organizations. As pointed out previously,
many of the newly appointed industrial top managers
had obtained their high positions not through party
membership and loyalty but on the basis of technical
and administrative competence. At the same time,
the political leadership expected enterprise party
organizations to continue to oversee, although not
interfere with, enterprise operations.

As could be expected, many enterprise managers
resented any kind of party tutelage in their daily
work, and this caused numerous misunderstandings and
complaints. During 1968, the official newspaper
Népszabadság published the following complaint of a
group of party members: "There is silence at enterprise party organization meetings. . . . It is use-
less to say anything, because managers do what they
want to. We, however, do not know what they do and
how they arrive at their decisions."[12]

Occasionally, the actions of the revitalized
labor unions also stirred up controversy in regard
to managerial independence. Although most enterprise
labor unions did not use their veto power over managerial decisions, they frequently limited the disciplinary powers of managers through collective-

bargaining agreements. Many enterprise labor-union
leaders considered it their duty to protect members
vigorously against disciplinary actions by managers,
even though, in many instances, this meant the con-
tinuation of undesirable work practices and the low-
ering of labor discipline.

Supply Problems

In an attempt to improve the material-supply
system, one of the weakest links in the pre-reform
economic order, NEM led to the abolishment of compulsory delivery contracts. During 1968-70, however,
to maintain the required equilibria in the various
macroeconomic balances, the reformers still had to
limit free trade in some items. Table 13 presents
the types of limitations used and the number of material and product groups to which the limitations
were applied.

From these data, it is clear that the number of
limitations and the number of material and product
groups to which the limitations applied were considerably reduced during the first three years of the
reform. Despite such favorable developments, however, expected over-all improvements in the material-
supply system did not become a reality. Manufacturers and distributors of many supply items still
enjoyed monopoly positions and, thus, could easily
dictate delivery terms and, frequently, price terms
to most buying enterprises. These enterprises, in
turn, strongly complained about the terms that they
were forced to accept.

Table 14 presents the findings of a study concerning the views of industrial-enterprise managers
about the general supply-contract terms before and
after NEM's implementation. With the exception of
managers in light and chemical industries, most managers polled believed that the general terms of supply
contracts were either unchanged or worse than during
the pre-reform years. Managers in almost all industries complained that it was impossible to close
preliminary contracts with suppliers, and managers
of smaller enterprises, especially, reported receiving
unfavorable treatment.

TABLE 13

Limits on Free Trade in Material-Supply System,
1968-70

Type of Limitation	Number of Supply Groups		
	1968	1969	1970
Central allocation	2	2	1
Import quotas	18	18	4
Buying quotas for production purposes	28	13	4
Buying quotas for retail trade purposes	13	8	10
Export quotas	22	10	10
Exclusive buyers and sellers	50	20	11
Minimum inventory requirements	0	0	3

Source: Otto Gadó, ed., Közgazdasági Szabályozó Rendszerünk Továbbfejlesztése (The Continued
Development of Our Economic Regulatory System) (Budapest: Közgazdasági és Jogi Könyvkiadó, 1970), p.
233.

Table 15 presents managerial views concerning
the timing of supply deliveries before and after the
reform by industrial and trading enterprises. As
can be seen from these data, most of the managers
polled believed that the timing of supply deliveries
did not improve relative to the pre-reform years.
Many managers pointed out that many suppliers maintained no inventory of the items requested and de-
manded a considerably higher price for special deliveries.

Some improvements, however, were reported by
the managers concerning the quality of materials and
products available. Table 16 summarizes managerial

TABLE 14

Managerial Views on General Supply-Contract Terms,
1969
(Per Cent)

Branch	Terms Improved	Terms Unchanged or Mixed	Terms Worsened
Chemical industry	33	33	33
Metallurgical industry	9	27	64
Construction industry	0	28	72
Light industry	41	30	29

Source: Kálmán Szabó, ed., A Vállalati Belsö
Mechanizmus Helyzete és Fejlödésének Föbb Vonásai
(Conditions of the Internal Enterprise Mechanism and
Its Major Developmental Features) (Budapest: A Mag-
yar Szocialista Munkáspárt Központi Bizottságának
Gazdaságpolitikai Osztálya, 1969), p. 79.

TABLE 15

Managerial Views on Timing of Supply Deliveries,
1969

Branch	Timing Improved	Timing Unchanged	Timing Worsened
Chemical industry	20	35	45
Metallurgical industry	8	54	38
Construction industry	0	43	57
Light industry	10	73	17

Source: Kálmán Szabó, ed., A Vállalati Belsö
Mechanizmus Helyzete és Fejlödésének Föbb Vonásai
(Conditions of the Internal Enterprise Mechanism and
Its Major Developmental Features) (Budapest: A Mag-
yar Szocialista Munkáspárt Központi Bizottságának
Gazdaságpolitikai Osztálya, 1969), p. 79.

TABLE 16

Managerial Views on Quality of Supplies, 1969
(Per Cent)

Branch	Quality Improved	Quality Un- changed	Quality Worsened
Chemical industry	18	77	5
Metallurgical industry	15	84	1
Construction industry	14	72	14
Light industry	6	85	9

Source: Kálmán Szabó, ed., A Vállalati Belsö
Mechanizmus Helyzete és Fejlödésének Föbb Vonásai
(Conditions of the Internal Enterprise Mechanism and
Its Major Developmental Features) (Budapest: A Mag-
yar Szocialista Munkáspárt Központi Bizottságának
Gazdaságpolitikai Osztálya, 1969), p. 80.

views on the topic of supply quality. Most of the
complaints were received from managers in the construction industry, because, as a result of a general
increase in world market prices, the foreign-trade
enterprises started to import less-expensive and,
thus, lower-quality materials.

The underlying reasons for the generally unsatisfactory conditions of the material-supply system were
very complex. The new financial rules, for example,
prompted many industrial and commercial enterprises
to minimize their inventories. The differences between the domestic and the foreign prices of certain
items made their export far more profitable than
their domestic marketing. Long-term trade contracts
with COMECON countries, which supply most of the materials used by Hungarian industry, made it difficult
to change the type or the quality of items imported.

Most important, however, the trading (wholesaling) enterprises did not improve the structure and efficiency of their distribution channels. As a consequence of financial and technical limitations, most trading enterprises used the time-consuming, burdensome channels already utilized during the pre-reform years. Although, under NEM, it would have been legally possible to develop new, shorter, multi-channel distribution systems, most trading enterprise managers did not seem willing to take the risk involved in implementing the necessary changes.

Pricing Problems

In developing the new price system, the reformers considered the average cost of production, demand conditions in domestic and foreign markets, and government preferences in terms of desirable social and economic objectives. Based on these considerations, the reformers introduced a mixed price system made up of fixed prices, prices subject to upper or both upper and lower limits, and completely free prices. It was expected that, gradually, most prices would fall into the last category and that, in time, effective price competition would develop in most markets.

During the first three years of NEM, the new price system, however, did not entirely fulfill the reformers' and the managers' expectations. By the end of 1970, only a few producer and consumer prices were completely free of any restrictions. Table 17 presents the distribution of producer prices among the different price categories. It is important to point out, however, that the 63.8 per cent of all producer prices listed as free in 1970 were, in practice, subject to contractual agreements between enterprises and, thus, were fixed for long periods of time and subject to official scrutiny.

Table 18 presents a similar distribution for consumer prices. As can be seen in both tables, during the first three years of the reform, the central authorities continued to subject most, especially consumer, prices to some form of restriction. In

TABLE 17

Distribution of Producer Prices, 1970[a]
(Per Cent)

Industry	Fixed Prices	Prices Subject to Upper Limits	Prices Subject to Upper and Lower Limits	Free Prices
Mining	4.7	62.6	0.2	32.5
Electrical energy	85.0	9.3	0.1	5.6
Metallurgical	0.5	84.8	0.6	14.1
Engineering	0.0	29.4	1.1	69.5
Construction	0.0	29.7	0.0	70.3
Chemical	17.8	29.3	0.2	52.7
Wood	0.0	18.9	0.0	81.1
Paper	0.0	3.1	0.0	96.9
Printing	0.0	8.6	41.1	50.3
Textile	0.0	13.9	0.0	86.1
Clothing	0.0	0.0	0.0	100.0
Food	4.9	7.5	4.7	82.9
Other	1.4	5.5	6.1	87.0
Handicraft and home	0.0	1.3	0.0	98.7
Total	5.8	28.7	1.7	63.8

[a]For both domestic and imported items.

Source: Figyèlö, April 28, 1971, p. 3.

TABLE 18

Distribution of Consumer Prices, 1970
(As Per Cent of Retail Turnover)

Type of Product	Fixed Prices	Prices Subject to Upper Limits	Prices Subject to Upper and Lower Limits	Free Prices
Food	30.1	34.6	21.6	13.7
Clothing	0.0	5.6	55.5	38.9
Technical and cultural	0.0	55.0	16.0	29.0
Heating materials	0.0	100.0	0.0	0.0
Chemical	20.3	44.1	0.0	33.6
Wood and paper	0.0	25.0	39.0	36.0
Building materials	11.0	55.1	0.0	33.9
Glass and china	0.0	15.2	0.0	84.8
Total	16.6	34.4	25.4	23.6

Source: Figyelö, April 28, 1971, p. 3.

addition, as illustrated in Chapter 2, the differences between producer and consumer prices remained large, and the reformers did not succeed in establishing realistic relationships between domestic and foreign prices.

Table 19 presents the deviation between domestic and foreign producer prices during the first year of the reform. To bridge the deviations between domestic and foreign prices, the central authorities had to utilize tariffs, taxes, and direct as well as indirect subsidies extensively. Importers of nonconsumer products, for example, received large subsidies during 1968-70, because, although foreign prices were

TABLE 19

Deviation Between Domestic and Foreign Producer
Prices, 1968
(Foreign Prices = 100)

Branch	Deviation from Nonsocialist Prices	Deviation from Socialist Prices
Electrical energy industry	+ 14.0	+ 14.0
Metallurgical industry	+ 2.5	+ 7.0
Engineering industry	+ 8.0	+ 7.2
Construction industry	− 2.0	− 7.5
Chemical industry	0.0	− 15.2
Light industry	+ 25.0	+ 4.2
Food industry	− 2.0	+ 6.7
Other	− 12.0	+ 4.0

Source: Figyelö, March 18, 1970, p. 3.

continually increasing, they were not permitted to
raise the domestic prices of imports. (Exporters
whose domestic cost of production exceeded the foreign price that they could obtain also received large
subsidies. In some cases, subsidized imported products had domestic substitutes that were sold abroad
under the export subsidy system.)

The central authorities wanted to shield the
domestic economy from worldwide inflationary tendencies. This policy of protecting the domestic economy
against foreign price influences prevented the possibility of an efficient allocation of resources.
It also put a tremendous burden on the central authorities, who had to neutralize foreign price movements through the continuous adjustment of financial
regulators, and on the central budget, out of which
the subsidies had to be paid. (In 1969, for example,
800 million forint were paid by the central authorities in the form of import subsidies to various enter-

prises; in 1970, this sum increased to well over 1
billion forint.) Furthermore, as pointed out previously, this protective policy, through the various
direct and indirect subsidies, significantly reduced
the role of profit as an enterprise success indicator.

The domestic pricing strategies of most enterprises were also rather disappointing. With a few
exceptions, enterprises that enjoyed a quasi- or full-
monopoly position, whenever legally possible, raised
both producer and consumer prices, regardless of market conditions. Their chief aim was to increase
profit and, thus, to create large profit-sharing and
development funds. Eventual cost savings were usually
not passed on to other enterprises or consumers in
the form of lower prices, but were absorbed in the
form of higher profit.

During the first year of the reform, it could
have been argued that most managers, not used to any
pricing authority and, perhaps, not fully understanding the functioning of the market place, were afraid
to use flexible pricing strategies and, thus, to reduce prices when market conditions justified such
action. During 1969-70, however, it became apparent
that most managers, although they understood pricing
theory by then, took full advantage of the seller's
market conditions and, whenever legally possible,
raised prices to realize their short-term objective
of larger profit-sharing and development funds.

Investment and Credit Problems

Under NEM, the National Bank and the Investment
Bank formed the cornerstone of the credit system.
The National Bank financed all variable (working)
capital needs, whereas the Investment Bank granted
fixed (investment) capital loans. As a general rule,
the central authorities expected all industrial enterprises to apply for loans from both institutions
only if temporary liquidity shortages occurred or if
the development fund was very small. Despite such
expectations, during the first three years of the
reform, most enterprises borrowed quite heavily from
both sources. Approximately 25 per cent of the

variable capital needs and more than 15 per cent of
the fixed capital requirements of industrial enterprises were met by the National Bank and the Investment Bank.

The annual credit directives specified the interest rates, the permissible repayment periods, and
the nature of preferred investment projects. During
1968-69, long-term loans were granted at a 5-per-cent
rate of interest before, and a 7-per-cent rate of
interest after, the completion of projects.[13] Me-
dium-range loans were extended, on the average, for
up to two years at an 8-per-cent rate of interest.
The experiences of the first three years have indicated that these interest rates did not reflect the
true scarcity value of capital in Hungary and, consequently, did not clear the credit market.

Investment activities were very extensive in
all sectors of the economy. During 1968-70, total
investment amounted to approximately 25 per cent of
gross national product (GNP).[14] About half the investment projects were planned and executed by the
central authorities, the other half by enterprise
managers. As a consequence of the relatively low
rates of interest, industry demand for investment
funds was very high. In 1968, for example, approximately one-third of the applicants had to be turned
down for lack of funds.

In 1969, demand for investment funds eased somewhat, because enterprises could, for the first time,
use their development funds, based on 1968 profits,
and because the central authorities limited long-
term credit to preferred projects. (This credit di-
rective discouraged many enterprise managers from
even applying for funds.) Furthermore, in 1968, many
enterprises overcommitted themselves and were thus
not eligible for additional credit in 1969.

The economic efficiency of most industrial investments was not satisfactory from an over-all
point of view. The depreciation and profit-alloca-
tion rules were applied equally to all enterprises,
regardless of the growth conditions in their indus-

tries. Consequently, enterprises in stagnating or
even decaying industries were required to generate
the same amount of depreciation and to allocate the
same proportion of profits to the development fund
as were enterprises in growth industries. (Enterprises could retain about 60 per cent of the annual
depreciation charges.) Such depreciation and profit-
allocation rules--together with the quasi- or full-
monopoly position of many enterprises, the ensuing
lack of competition, and the generous subsidy policies
of the central authorities--enabled many enterprises
that should have curtailed, or, at least, not expanded,
operations to invest and expand.

The composition of most industrial investment
projects did not meet the long-range needs of the
Hungarian economy either. Not enough investments
were directed toward improvement of the neglected
infrastructure, and most enterprises tried to increase their production capacity through the building
of new plants. (About 60 per cent of all new investments involved construction projects.) Newly purchased machines were used chiefly to equip new facilities and not to replace the old, frequently worn-out
machines of many existing plants. This resulted in
the postponement of much-needed technological improvements in many industries.

The extensive investment activities of industrial
enterprises and the shortage of funds put the National
Bank and the Investment Bank into influential positions. The numerous credit applications were evaluated by the banks chiefly on the basis of the proposed
repayment period. This and other stringent credit
requirements, such as the size and the liquidity of
the collateral, prompted many managers to complain
that the government bureaucracy of the pre-reform
years had been replaced by bank bureaucracy. The
tough credit requirements displeased not only enterprise managers but many other members of Hungarian
society as well. A well-known author, for example,
charged that, under NEM, "the Hungarian National
Bank took over, from the cultural authorities, the
direction of the country's cultural life."[15]

The extensive investment activities also put
great upward pressure on the prices of most investment goods. Table 20 presents the price index of investment goods, broken down by major categories for
1968-70. As can be seen, the prices of construction
goods and of imported machines rose considerably during 1968. This was the consequence of the great demand for construction, in general, and the increase
of machine prices in foreign markets, as well as the
application of the new foreign-trade price multiplier.
During 1969-70, except for construction, prices in
most other categories tended to remain relatively
stable.

The planning and execution of investment projects
and new economic activities at the enterprise level
left much to be desired. Most managers were not well
versed in the preparation of financial plans and had
little experience in the application of economic
analysis to investment decision-making. Well-trained
staff specialists were in short supply, and, without
realistic advice, many managers tended, optimistically

TABLE 20

Price Index of Major Investment-Goods Categories,
1968-70
(Previous Year = 100)

Year	Construction	Domestic Machines	Imported Machines	Other
1968	115.6	109.5	115.4	104.0
1969	104.0	100.1	101.4	101.9
1970[a]	104.1	100.9	99.4	101.3

[a]Estimated.

Source: Figyelö, March 31, 1971, p. 5.

to overestimate expected future revenues generated
by the planned investments. To satisfy the lending
requirements of both the National Bank and the Investment Bank, the expected repayment period was emphasized over all aspects of the planned projects.

As a consequence of poor planning, financial decisions were frequently made in a crisis atmosphere,
especially since investment cost overruns occurred
very frequently. During 1970, for example, more than
50 per cent of all investments incurred unexpected
cost overruns ranging from 3 per cent to 40 per cent
of the value of the projects.[16] As could be expected,
such undesirable developments called for immediate
remedial action, which put a great burden on enterprise managers, the Investment Bank, the National
Bank, and the supervisory branch ministries. Frequently, no immediate financial aid was available,
and, consequently, numerous investment projects remained unfinished.

Poor financial management and investment decision-making were, among other factors, partially responsible for the undesirable increase in enterprise
inventories during the first three years of the reform. The delayed completion of investment projects
was especially important in this respect. Table 21
shows the relationship of inventories to GNP during
1968-70. As can be seen, after a high rate of inventory increase during 1968, the year 1969 showed
considerable improvement. In 1970, however, inventories again grew at a faster rate, primarily because
of an increase in industrial and commercial inventories.

Table 22 presents a summary of inventory changes
in the industrial sector of the economy. In contrast
with the past, however, the 1970 increase in industrial inventories--especially those in the chemical,
engineering, and light industries--was not entirely
undesirable. Increases in these industries were
caused chiefly by the building up of exceptionally
low inventories, changes in product mixes, increased
demand in the market place, and increased imports to
improve the domestic material-supply system.

TABLE 21

Relationship Between GNP and Inventories, 1968-70
(Billion Forint, 1971 Prices)

Item	1968	1969	1970
GNP	249.2	278.9	297.2
Inventories	16.9	10.6	14.8
Inventories (as per cent of GNP)	6.78	3.80	4.98

Source: Figyelö, July 14, 1971, p. 3.

TABLE 22

Inventory Changes in Industry, 1968-70
(Billion Forint, 1971 Prices)

Item	1968	1969	1970
Industrial sector, without food industry	+ 9.3	+ 3.9	+ 6.5

Source: Figyelö, July 14, 1971, p. 3.

As could be expected, poor financial management
over an extended period of time caused survival problems for several enterprises.[17] During the first
three years of NEM, approximately fifty industrial
enterprises had their bank credit limited for various
lengths of time. About six enterprises had to be
completely refinanced by the central authorities,
four needed reorganization, and twenty-four used
other methods of solving their financial problems.
In addition, twenty-one enterprises overcommitted
their development funds and could not meet the financial obligations incurred through the funds. To

ensure their continued survival, the central authorities provided direct financial aid to three enterprises, eight had to utilize their reserve funds, and
all the others had to change investment plans.

The composition and economic efficiency of investments are crucial to any economic system. Consequently, the investment and credit problems of NEM
were among the most serious ones during 1968-70.

Employment and Labor-Relations Problems

One basic objective of NEM was an increase in
over-all industrial efficiency through improved labor
productivity. To accomplish this objective, the reformers, through the new Labor Code and associated
regulations, considerably enlarged managerial authority in the area of employment and labor relations.
During 1968-70, however, none of the expected improvements was realized. In 1968 and 1969, labor
productivity virtually stagnated, increasing only
1.1 per cent and 0.4 per cent, respectively. Although
the situation improved in 1970, when labor productivity went up 6.8 per cent, the average annual increase in labor productivity during the first three
years of NEM was unsatisfactory. This undesirable
development was accompanied, and probably partially
caused, by a lack of improvement in industrial discipline and a very high rate of labor mobility.

The low level of labor productivity and industrial discipline during the first three years of
NEM was generated partially by historical factors and
partially by certain features of the reform. Historically, the transformation of Hungary from an essentially agricultural to an industrial society has
taken place only since the mid- to late 1940's.
This transformation was accompanied by a large-scale
transfer of unskilled and poorly educated agricultural
workers into industrial enterprises where, within a
relatively short period of time, they had to adjust
to a new way of life. (In 1968, for example, 37 per
cent of the industrial labor force had less than
eight years of basic schooling.[18])

The majority of Hungary's current skilled-labor
pool are former agricultural workers who, as a consequence of the shortage of training facilities and
the pressure of time during the early 1950's, received
only limited instruction in new technical skills.
Work experience, in most cases, did not improve, but,
rather, aggravated the situation, because, as time
went on, poor working habits and techniques became
even more firmly established. In addition, as pointed
out previously, in many industries, skilled workers
had to use old, worn-out machinery and equipment and
thus had difficulties in improving performance.

Despite the great demand for both skilled and
semiskilled workers, the training of industrial labor
slowed down during the first two years of NEM. Table
23 presents this trend, relative to the pre-reform
years, in summary form. It was only in 1970 that the
central authorities seriously considered the problems
of training industrial workers. The Ministry of
Labor developed a plan according to which, in the

TABLE 23

Number of Industrial Workers Trained, 1965-69
(Thousands)

Year	Skilled Workers[a]	Semiskilled Workers	Continued Training of Skilled and Semiskilled Workers
1965	35.3	60.3	39.6
1966	27.2	56.8	47.4
1967	25.9	74.1	44.6
1968	24.1	65.8	39.5
1969	27.5	71.0	40.0

[a]Includes driver training.

Source: Figyelö, June 2, 1971, p. 1.

future, industrial workers would be trained on a
partly voluntary and partly compulsory basis every
five to eight years. (In April, 1971, the government
issued two official training decrees based on this
plan.) The ministry recommended that such training
should be based on general educational subjects,
technical skills, and socialist ideology.

   In addition to the historical factors, the problems of low labor productivity and industrial discipline were further aggravated by the average wage
control system introduced as a major feature of NEM.
The system was designed to combat cost inflation and
to prevent the development of unemployment. According to the system, before taxable annual enterprise
profit was divided among the profit-sharing and development funds, it was augmented, for accounting
purposes, by 100 per cent of that part of the total
annual wage bill that was in excess of the amount
permitted by the average reference wage. (The average reference wage was the same as the total 1967
wage bill of each enterprise divided by the number of
employees.) This sum was then deducted from the
posttax profit-sharing fund.

   In other words, an increase in the total annual
wage bill over the amount permitted by the average
reference wage reduced the total amount of profit
available for distribution to managers and other employees. Under such conditions, it was understandable that the average wage control system served as
a strong incentive to keep the annual enterprise
wage bill as low as possible. To accomplish this
objective, managers tended not only to retain but,
actively, to seek low-wage semiskilled and unskilled
labor instead of high-wage skilled workers. (In
many enterprises, managers also tended to make up
the production loss resulting from the decrease in
the work week from 48 hours to 44 hours through the
employment of new workers.)

   As could be expected, such employment policies
put great pressure on the labor market. The historically conditioned shortage of skilled workers
was augmented by the great demand for semiskilled

and unskilled workers. Many enterprises that, as a
result of past official employment policies, already
had a considerable overstaffing problem hired additional low-wage and low-skill workers. Such widespread employment policies, coupled with a high degree
of labor mobility and the desire of managers to retain workers at almost any cost, had a very negative
effect on industrial discipline and labor productivity.

The central authorities soon recognized that the
average wage control system created a conflict between the short-run interests of managers and the
long-run interests of the economy. Therefore, to
reduce this conflict, on January 1, 1970, they changed
the system to require that only 70 per cent of the
excess amount of the 1970 wage bill over the 1969
wage bill had to be charged against the profit-sharing
fund and not the entire amount. (Thus, the 1969 average reference wage replaced the 1967 average reference
wage as the new standard of wage adjustments.)

Furthermore, to control the staff-increasing
tendency of most industrial enterprises, the new
rules instructed managers to deduct one-third of the
increase in the annual wage bill caused by the addition of new employees from the pretax profit-sharing
fund and to transfer this amount to the central budget. In contrast, enterprises that reduced their
staff received a reduction in tax obligations.

The positive effects of the new average wage
control system on enterprise employment policies,
and, thus, on industrial discipline and labor productivity, were considerable. Labor productivity in
1970--as opposed to 1968 and 1969, when it virtually
stagnated--went up 6.8 per cent. Since the number of
new workers employed increased less than 1 per cent
in 1970, most of this improvement was the result of
more-efficient enterprise operations. Nevertheless,
labor relations in general and discipline in particular were still not satisfactory.

Well-trained labor-relations specialists were
in short supply. (The term "labor-relations special-

ist" is used in a very general sense. It includes
specialists in time and motion studies, organizational
experts, and salary and wage analysts.) According
to one study, for example, in 1970, only about 10 per
cent of the approximately 20,000 labor-relations
specialists employed in Hungarian industry had an advanced degree in a field related to economics.[19]
About 60 per cent finished high school, whereas 30
per cent never received any education beyond the required eight years. Furthermore, this study also
found that one labor-relations specialist, on the
average, had to deal with 268 workers.

Most managers did not consider labor relations
an important enterprise function. In many cases, the
work of the labor-relations departments was limited
to the routine matters of checking employment refer-
ences and computing wages and salaries. Consequently,
enterprise labor requirements were not well planned,
work procedures were not systematically reviewed,
many job descriptions were dated or unclear, and the
in-plant training of both skilled and unskilled workers was neglected. Furthermore, most enterprises
did not have a well-structured and consistent wage
policy; thus, the relationship between wages and individual work performance was not very strong.

Wages and salaries were determined, within the
official guidelines, in an egalitarian manner and
thus could not be used as an effective motivator.
Probably as a result of the unpleasant experiences
during the pre-reform years, the number of industrial
workers paid on a performance basis decreased 6.1
per cent during 1967-69, whereas the number of workers paid on a time basis increased 6.7 per cent.[20]
In most enterprises, poor work performance in general
and excessively wasteful production in particular
were not penalized in the form of reduced wages or
other sanctions. Managers were afraid that disciplinary actions would cause workers to quit their jobs.

The problem of employee discipline and labor
productivity was probably also affected by the behavior and attitudes of the managers themselves, who,
frequently, were quite lax in their dealings with

other enterprises, suppliers, and customers. According to one study, 55 per cent of the products put on the market by light industry during the last quarter of 1969 were of an unacceptable quality by official standards.[21] Developments of a similar nature, unless the central authorities found out about them, were frequently covered up as fully and as long as possible by many managers, who, out of misguided solidarity, tended to protect each other. Such managerial behavior, however, did not always go unnoticed by the workers and supporting personnel, who, quite understandably, were negatively affected by it.

Incentive Problems

During the first two years of the reform, the major feature of the new incentive system was the profit-sharing plan based on a job classification scheme developed by the central authorities. As pointed out in Chapter 2, the jobs in each industrial enterprise were divided into three categories. Top managers--such as the general manager and his deputies, the chief engineer, the controller, the heads of large sections, and economic and technical consultants--were in Category I. Middle managers--such as heads of small sections and departments and technical, legal, and economic experts--belonged to Category II. Finally, administrative and other supporting personnel, as well as workers, made up Category III.

The maximum profit share that could be paid to individual employees in the different categories was determined by the central authorities as a percentage of the average annual salary of all employees in the given category. Under this system, top managers could receive 80 per cent; middle managers, 50 per cent; and supporting personnel and workers, 15 per cent.

As mentioned in Chapter 3, the allocation of the largest profit share to top managers met with strong resentment on the part of many Hungarian citizens. Industrial workers, in particular, were dissatisfied because they believed that top managers were well paid to begin with and that, therefore, the new

arrangement represented a breach of socialist morality. Workers also suspected that managers were reluctant to increase wages because, through the average wage control system, any such increase would
considerably reduce managerial profit shares.

The widespread resentment and suspicions, however, were not entirely justified. In 1968, for example, total managerial incomes, relative to the pre-
reform years, increased less than 5 per cent, and,
in some industries--such as engineering and metal-
lurgy--they actually decreased. During 1970-71, however, managerial incomes increased considerably.
Many people, and, again, especially industrial workers, were also disturbed by the decrease in 1969,
from the 1968 level, in the total amount of profit
shares paid throughout Hungarian industry. In 1968,
700 million forint were used to increase wages and
6.3 billion forint were paid in the form of profit
shares, for a total of 7 billion forint.[22] In 1969,
as a result of slightly changed enterprise wage policies, 2.7 billion forint were used to increase wages
and 5.9 billion forint were paid in the form of profit
shares, for a total of 8.6 billion forint.

This represented an increase of more than 20
per cent over the total amount that managers, employees, and workers earned in 1968. Despite this
increase, however, many workers were disgruntled,
because they knew that, although profit shares dis-
tributed in 1969 decreased, total enterprise profits
earned during the same year were up 8.6 per cent
over 1968. Under such conditions, workers considered
the wage increases received during 1969 a just and
well-deserved reward but felt that the decrease in
profit shares was unfair.

The application of the profit-sharing system as
a motivator left much to be desired. In most cases,
profit allocations were made by top managers alone,
and, thus, the immediate supervisors of most employees and workers had little influence over the size
of individual profit shares. Furthermore, top managers tended not to differentiate between employees
in the same position on the basis of the quality of

work performed or loyalty shown. It happened that,
in many enterprises, an employee or worker going
through the motions of work in a slow and disinter-
ested manner received the same profit share as did
another employee or worker who, through his innovative behavior, made a much greater contribution to
enterprise objectives.

Managers justified this practice by claiming
that it was very difficult to measure, consistently
and fairly, the contributions made by different individuals. The difficulty of such measurement notwithstanding, it seemed that most managers were
reluctant to use their differentiating authority because they did not want to create dissatisfaction
among employees. Most managers tended to believe
that an egalitarian approach to the distribution of
profit shares was the best security against possible
conflicts resulting from differing individual shares,
however well deserved.

The central authorities were well aware of the
dissatisfaction caused by the profit-sharing system
and, consequently, as of January 1, 1970, fundamentally changed it. The job classification scheme and
the associated maximum profit-share specifications
were abolished. Under the new system, top managers,
middle managers, and supporting personnel, as well
as workers, could all receive the same profit share
at the end of the year.

Top managers were instructed not to distribute
individual profit shares on an egalitarian basis,
but, rather, to reward good individual performance
in an outstanding manner. To make managers less dependent on annual profit shares, their basic salaries
were raised and new emphasis was put on the payment
of special bonuses to top managers by the supervisory
authorities, such as the branch ministries. The
size of the bonus was to be determined by a special
formula based on both the enterprise wage fund and
profit, or, in other words, on enterprise efficiency.

The 1970 changes undoubtedly reduced employee
dissatisfaction with the profit-sharing system. As

a result of the changes, the financial incentive system functioned much better than during the two previous years. Nevertheless, it still did not entirely
fulfill the reformers' expectations. Most managers
did not change their egalitarian attitudes as quickly
and as fundamentally as they were expected to do.
Most enterprise wage, salary, and profit-sharing
plans were not combined into an effective motivating
program.

It should, however, be emphasized that it was
not easy to adjust the financial incentive system
according to the new rules in a short period of time.
Many employees and workers were used to the egalitarian approach and considered profit shares an almost permanent part of their total income. Consequently, the introduction and application of a more
differentiated system called for a good understanding
of human behavior in formal organizations in general
and motivation of employees in particular. Most Hungarian managers, however, lacked a solid background
in the human aspects of management and, thus, were
not prepared to deal effectively with the issues
caused by the introduction of such an important organizational change. (Recently, however, more and
more emphasis has been put on the behavioral aspects
of management by the central authorities and by managerial training institutions.)

Foreign-Trade Problems

Hungary, like all other small countries, increasingly faces the problem of a narrowing range of
products that it can manufacture and sell competitively in world markets. At the same time, the
range of products that it has to import is widening
to meet the increasingly sophisticated demand of
its producers and consumers. Consequently, to improve its competitiveness in world markets and to
earn enough foreign exchange to finance needed imports, Hungary has to rely more and more on the international division of labor and on economic cooperation with both the socialist and nonsocialist
world.

The foreign-trade system of NEM was designed to accomplish these objectives. As could be expected, however, during the first three years of the reform, the transformation of the Hungarian economy from an essentially closed to an open one was impeded by several problems. For example, as discussed previously, the reformers did not succeed in their attempt to establish realistic relationships between domestic and foreign prices. The central authorities tried to bridge the deviations between domestic and foreign prices through the foreign-trade price multiplier and other financial regulators, such as tariffs, taxes, and subsidies. (During 1968-70, the foreign-trade price multiplier stood at 60 forint to U.S. $1 and at 40 forint to 1 Soviet ruble.) By the end of 1970, however, it was clear that they had not entirely accomplished their objectives and that the continuous adjustments and subsidies needed to keep the equalizing mechanism functioning were putting a great burden on both the central authorities and the central budget.

International-trade experts, notably Balassa, have argued that the foreign-trade price multiplier was overvalued and that it, together with export subsidies, tended to freeze exports in their past, inefficient form.[23] Furthermore, Balassa pointed out, an overvalued foreign-trade price multiplier encourages imports for which domestic prices have to be continually adjusted through the numerous financial regulators mentioned above. According to a Hungarian economist, the foreign-trade price multiplier, during 1968, was overvalued by about 15 per cent relative to the U.S. dollar and about 10 per cent relative to the Soviet ruble.[24]

At the same time, Hungary's terms of trade with its foreign partners improved. Relative to the socialist countries, the improvement was slight; relative to the nonsocialist countries, however, it was considerable. Table 24 summarizes the foreign-trade price index and the terms of trade relative to both groups of countries during 1968-70. The improvements in the terms of trade in general and in those with the nonsocialist (dollar-trade) countries in partic-

TABLE 24

Foreign-Trade Price Index and Terms of Trade,
1968-70
(As Per Cent of 1965 Price Level)

Type of Countries	1968	1969	1970
Socialist countries			
Imports	93.7	94.1	95.0
Exports	95.0	95.4	96.1
Terms of trade	101.4	101.4	101.2
Nonsocialist countries			
Imports	94.3	97.2	102.7
Exports	92.9	99.6	108.8
Terms of trade	98.5	102.5	105.9

Source: Figyelö, April 21, 1971, p. 7.

ular, the favorable over-all balance-of-payments developments, and the desire of the central authorities
to stimulate competition and to offer a better product choice in the domestic markets all resulted in
a large increase of consumer-goods imports from both
the socialist and the nonsocialist countries.

The prices of these products were essentially
"free" in the domestic market, but had to be set by
the trading enterprises on the basis of the appropriate foreign-trade price multiplier and the other
financial regulators, such as tariffs and taxes. As
could be expected, this policy resulted in very high
domestic prices for most products and relatively high
profits for the trading enterprises. For example,
the clothing trading (wholesaling) enterprises obtained a 5-9-per-cent profit margin on imports from
socialist countries and a 6-14-per-cent profit margin
on imports from nonsocialist countries--this at a

time when the central authorities considered a 3.5-
per-cent profit margin as reasonable on such imports.

Consumer reaction was predictable. Most Hungarians considered the price of imports from nonsocialist countries, relative to the price of the
available domestic substitutes, far too high and thus
purchased less of such products than was expected.
Although the prices of imports from socialist countries were more moderate, supply inflexibilities
(despite the absence of quantity restrictions since
1968) and the occasional low quality of such imports
also discouraged consumers from buying. Consequently,
the objectives of the central authorities concerning
increased imports were not accomplished. On the contrary, the high prices of many imports frequently
encouraged the manufacturers of domestic substitutes
to raise their prices whenever possible and, thus, to
put a strong upward pressure on the domestic price
level.

To overcome these undesirable developments, the
central authorities in 1969 removed restrictions on
consumer-goods imports from ten developing nations,
including the United Arab Republic, Tunisia, and
Yugoslavia. The same year, the domestic sales tax
on many imported products was reduced. Nevertheless,
conditions in the consumer-goods market did not improve. Consequently, as of January 1, 1970, the central authorities further modified the rules governing
imports. The consumer sales tax on all imports from
socialist countries was abolished, and the sales tax
on imports from nonsocialist countries was reduced
(in that the tax had to be computed on the posttariff
wholesale price of products).

Trading enterprises were instructed to observe
the centrally determined profit-margin guidelines and
not to deviate from them by more than 30 per cent
annually in the case of imported clothing items and
20 per cent in the case of all other products except
food, tropical fruits, and other such items imported
for the purpose of improving domestic product choice.
Finally, the foreign-exchange limitations on the importation of coffee, lemon, fish filet, and spices

were eliminated. As a consequence of these new rules,
consumer-goods imports from both socialist and nonsocialist countries increased considerably in 1970
and thus enabled the central authorities to reduce
tension somewhat in the domestic consumer-goods markets. Table 25 presents a summary of these developments.

Foreign-trade developments in Hungary during
1968-70 were also seriously impeded by certain characteristics of COMECON. The influence of COMECON on
the long-range objectives of NEM in general and Hungarian foreign-trade objectives in particular is significant, because more than half of Hungarian exports
go to its fellow member countries and more than half
of Hungarian imports are obtained from them. Foreign-
trade relationships between COMECON countries are
still governed by long-term, bilateral trade agreements. In working out agreements, partners attempt
to balance their exports and imports--that is, imports are not determined by cost comparisons but by
the ability to market exports in the partner country.
As a result of this, both the efficiency of production and the volume of trade are reduced and the international division of labor is impaired.

Furthermore, the domestic price systems do not
reflect true economic conditions, and the deviations

TABLE 25

Retail Turnover and Retail-Wholesale Inventories of
Consumer Products, 1969-70
(As Per Cent of Previous Year)

Year	Retail Turnover	Retail-Wholesale Inventories
1969	109.6	103.3
1970	113.6	119.4

Source: Figyelö, February 24, 1971, p. 3.

between domestic and foreign prices continue to be
significant. Frequently, foreign-trade prices are
applicable only to trade with a particular partner
at a certain point in time. The "transfer ruble,"
introduced as a first approximation of a common currency in 1964, did not fulfill the member countries'
expectations. For the transfer ruble to be an effective medium of exchange, it would have to be the common denominator of production costs and national
currencies convertible regionally at their approximate
purchasing power. Such conditions, however, still
do not exist in the COMECON countries, and, consequently, multilateral trade and integration--that is,
an effective international division of labor and
economic cooperation between the member countries--
are still a long way off.

From this brief discussion of the major characteristics of foreign-trade relationships between the
COMECON countries, it is clear that the long-range
success of NEM is largely dependent upon solving the
above-mentioned problems. It is understandable that,
during recent COMECON meetings, the Hungarian representatives have emphasized the need for an immediate
start toward the establishment of more-realistic
trade relationships between the member countries.
The issues involved, however, are not only economic
but also political; thus, the Hungarian reformers
have a very long and hard road ahead of them.

The foreign-trade activities of both the specialized foreign-trade commercial enterprises and the
internationally involved Hungarian industrial enterprises were generally satisfactory during 1968-70.
True, in 1969, managers of some industrial enterprises seemed to have ignored the domestic markets
in favor of the more lucrative export markets and,
thus, probably contributed to the tensions that prevailed in the domestic industrial (investment) and
consumer markets. This, however, was probably less
of a problem than were some of the difficulties oc-
curring in the conduct of foreign trade at both the
commercial and the industrial enterprise levels.

As discussed in Chapter 2, the working relationships between the specialized foreign-trade commercial enterprises and the industrial enterprises could
take several different forms. They could be based
on long-term partnership contracts or on an agent,
consignee, shipper, or marketing-representative basis. During the first three years of the reform, the
consignee-type arrangement dominated. In 1970, for
example, 68 per cent of the ruble-trade and 66 per
cent of the dollar-trade imports took the form of
profit-sharing or commission consignments.[25] Corresponding shares for exports were 43 per cent of the
ruble trade and 31 per cent of the dollar trade.

A little over 50 per cent of all import and
about 15 per cent of all export consignments, however, lacked the advantages of continuous trade relationships and were conducted on a case-by-case
basis.[26] This type of relationship introduced an
element of uncertainty into the foreign-trade activities of many industrial enterprises and prevented
the commercial enterprises from undertaking comprehensive market research studies for their clients
and, in general, from developing systematic and comprehensive long-range marketing strategies. In addition, some industrial enterprises refrained from
specifying price limits to the commercial enterprises,
which tended to cause misunderstandings and arguments
over the final price.

The financing of foreign trade with nonsocialist
(dollar-trade) partners at the enterprise level also
had certain shortcomings. During 1969, for example,
about 25 per cent of Hungarian exports to nonsocialist countries were based on direct cash payments,
whereas the remainder was financed through other
means.[27] Although short-term (3-6 months) credit
financing is widely used today in the international
dollar-trade market, only about 15 per cent of all
Hungarian exports to this market, during 1968-70,
were based on such financial arrangements, and almost
half the bills involved were discounted by the Hungarian National Bank.[28]

At a time when Hungary is trying to become an
important exporter of selected capital equipment--
such as machines and transportation equipment--to the
nonsocialist world, the unwillingness to offer short-
term credit arrangements can be, among other factors,
a serious competitive handicap, because most international buyers of capital equipment want such financing. Furthermore, as a consequence of not
utilizing the available international financing methods, most Hungarian enterprises involved in foreign
trade have unnecessarily burdened themselves with
self-financing.

It could be argued that, during the pre-reform
years, the rigid foreign-trade policies of the central authorities made extensive participation of
Hungarian enterprises in international capital markets impossible. Under NEM, this argument is no
longer valid because the central authorities actively
encourage such international involvement. (In May
and June, 1971, for example, the Hungarian National
Bank, for the first time in many years, offered a
$25-million bond issue for sale in the Western Euro-
pean capital markets. More than eighty financial
institutions from England, France, the Federal Republic of Germany, and other countries purchased the
bonds.) To most Hungarian economists, it is clear
that the long-range objective of an increased international division of labor and economic cooperation
can be accomplished only if all Hungarian industrial
and commercial enterprises involved in foreign trade
explore, in a more systematic and consistent fashion,
the opportunities offered by the international financial markets.

MANAGERIAL PROBLEMS

The problems discussed below were caused chiefly
by managerial attitudes and behavior generated by
the political, economic, social, and cultural environment of Hungary. As a consequence of their essentially historical nature, the central authorities
could not even attempt to correct these problems
through the relatively simple technique of adjusting

certain features of NEM or issuing new guidelines.
Thus, the correction of these problems had to be approached through the difficult, time-consuming, and
very costly procedure of managerial education and
retraining.

Irregular Production Patterns

As noted in Chapter 1, during the pre-reform
years, Hungarian industrial managers tended to gear
all enterprise activities to the long-run maximiza-
tion of managerial bonuses. To accomplish this objective, they had to meet the centrally designated,
quarterly enterprise production targets on time. As
a consequence of the inadequate material-supply system, occasional changes in production assignments,
planning errors, and various types of intra-enterprise
operational problems, managers, around the end of
every third month, had to resort to storming practices to meet production target dates. As could be
expected, this led to excessive overtime, poor-quality
products, occasional accidents, and other undesirable
side effects.

Under NEM, most of the environmental factors
that caused the irregular production patterns were
eliminated. In addition, managers were encouraged
to formulate a long-term orientation and to develop
their trade contacts with other industrial and commercial enterprises on the basis of their own production possibilities and demand requirements. Nevertheless, during the first three years of the reform,
it became apparent that the majority of industrial
enterprises continued to follow the old pattern.
Figure 4 presents the pattern of industrial production on a monthly basis for the years 1968-70.

As in the past, the uneven industrial production
patterns put a great burden on enterprise quality in-
spectors, packers, shippers, and administrative personnel engaged in the preparation of documents and
bills. This usually results in superficial quality
inspection, hasty shipping and billing procedures,
and a considerable amount of overtime. Table 26
presents a breakdown of industrial overtime on a

FIGURE 4

Monthly Pattern of Industrial
Production, 1968-70

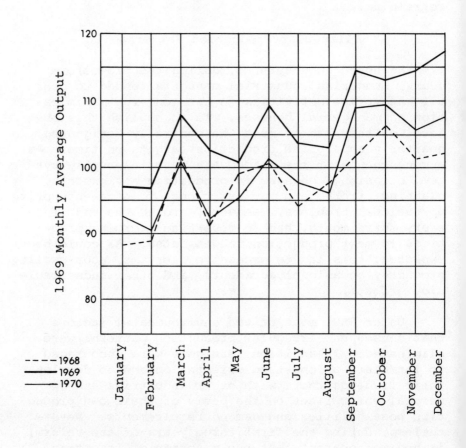

Source: Lászlóné Tüü, "Az Ipari Termelés
Ütemessége, 1968-70" (Industrial Production Patterns,
1968-70), Gazdaság, March, 1970, p. 75.

TABLE 26

Industrial Overtime, 1968-70[a]
(As Per Cent of Total Labor Hours)

Year	Yearly Average	March	June	September	December
1968	1.7	1.5	2.0	1.9	2.4
1969	2.2	1.9	2.3	2.4	3.1
1970	3.1	2.9	3.3	3.3	3.5

[a]Excludes food industry.

Source: Lászlóné Tüü, "Az Ipari Termelés Ütemessége, 1968-70" (Industrial Production Patterns, 1968-70), Gazdaság, March, 1970, p. 81.

quarterly basis for the first three years of the reform. Although overtime represented 1.7 per cent of total industrial labor hours in 1968, this figure increased to 2.2 per cent in 1969 and 3.1 per cent in 1970.

In addition to the number of hours worked, the irregular production patterns also affected the trading relationships between industrial and commericial enterprises. Both the domestic and the foreign-trade commercial enterprises usually received large, quarterly product shipments from the industrial enterprises. This forced the commercial enterprises to increase their inventories to an uneconomically high level suddenly and, after inventories were gradually depleted, frequently to run out of products for awhile.

Furthermore, the irregular production patterns tended to create transportation bottlenecks, delayed the completion of investment projects, and, thus,

caused cost overruns. Other enterprises were forced
to engage in storming practices. The development of
systematic long-range marketing strategies for both
domestic and foreign-trade commercial enterprises
was made very difficult. Finally, the irregular production patterns affected labor morale. In many industrial enterprises, work loads were quite uneven,
with not enough work at the beginning of each quarter,
but a considerable amount of overtime required at
the end.

As pointed out previously, most of the environmental factors that caused irregular production patterns during the pre-reform years were eliminated
under NEM. The reasons for similar developments during 1968-70 were, therefore, most likely caused by
the continued short-term outlook of most industrial
managers. Managers, although discouraged by the central authorities from doing so, rarely looked beyond
one or two years at the most. Their efforts were
concentrated on the creation of large profit-sharing
and development funds, and, since the size of both
funds depended on the amount of annual profits, managers scheduled most enterprise activities on a calen-
dar basis over a period of one to two years, regardless of the long-term effects of such behavior upon
the national economy and upon their enterprises.

Inadequate Planning and
Risk-Taking

As could be expected, the short-term outlook of
most industrial managers strongly affected the quality
of over-all enterprise planning. Most types of enterprise plans--such as marketing, labor, technical,
and expansion plans for both the short run and the
long run--were either nonexistent or vague. They
were frequently based on unsatisfactory planning
premises and unsubstantiated profit expectations.

As mentioned earlier, sometimes the information
disseminated by the central authorities was not comprehensive and systematic enough to permit the development of good planning premises. Nevertheless, the
relatively low quality of enterprise planning was

not caused by this factor, but by the short-term outlook of industrial managers, many of whom believed
that, since their enterprises operated in a seller's
market, there was no need for good planning except
in the area of production.

Another negative effect of the managers' short-
term outlook on enterprise performance was the unwillingness of most managers to take risks. In
dealing with the futurity of current decisions, the
majority of managers tended to overemphasize the
probability and magnitude of losses. A study concerning the risk-taking attitudes of industrial managers, for example, found that, in the important areas
of research and development, organizational development, introduction of new products, application of
new technology, capacity expansion, and inventory
management, only 33 per cent of the managers polled
believed that their risk-taking attitude was satisfactory.[29]

Most of the managers interviewed pointed out
that the lack of risk-taking was the result of the
seller's market conditions in many industries, the
absence of a direct relationship between risk-taking
and the economic position of the enterprise, and,
finally, the fear of financial losses for which managers could be penalized in the form of reduced salaries. All are essentially short-term considerations.

Inadequate Marketing

The short-term outlook of most industrial managers also affected the performance of the marketing
function. In the past, marketing in Hungary was
considered a "necessary evil" that did not merit the
same attention as did other problems of economic
growth.[30] This negative attitude was based partially
on ideological grounds and partially on the realities
of economic life during the pre-reform years. The
ideological basis was Karl Marx's contention that
capital invested in trade (marketing) is part of the
dead expenses of the capitalist economic system.[31]

The realities of economic life manifested themselves in the management of the Hungarian economy
through a highly centralized, bureaucratic planning
system in which the market place did not perform its
function of allocating goods and services. Thus,
marketing, as it was understood and practiced in
capitalist economies, had little relevance to the
kind of marketing activity necessary for such economic conditions. The introduction of the market
place, the emphasis on competition, and the new policy
of satisfying consumer demand to the highest possible
degree, however, changed all this, and marketing became a very important enterprise function.

As pointed out above, the early debates concerning the nature and role of marketing under NEM
did not result in a set of propositions that could
be used as decision-making guides by managers. Consequently, it was, to some extent, understandable
that the marketing activities of many industrial enterprises were inadequate. Recent studies, for example, have shown that many Hungarian industrial managers tend to confuse marketing with market research
and the organizational issues involved in selling.[32]
Undoubtedly, in an economy where marketing was ignored for many years, organizational issues can be
very important; but, to confuse such issues with the
essence of modern marketing--namely, the long-term
consumer orientation of all enterprise activities--
is a serious error.

Furthermore, although most industrial managers
identified the effective development of competitive
and up-to-date products as one of their most current
pressing problems, most of them did not consider the
development of such products to be a long-range marketing strategy issue. A study of the Economic Research Institute, for example, found that only about
20 per cent of all industrial enterprises planned to
improve their marketing efforts over the 1971-75 period. Instead, they believed that such development
was chiefly the short-term job of engineers who work
in the research and development laboratories and on
the production lines.

The short-term outlook of industrial managers
and the resulting inadequate performance of marketing
resulted in frequent clashes between the interests
of managers and consumers. As mentioned above, managers frequently raised the uncontrolled prices of
products, regardless of market conditions and consumer reactions. Occasionally, because of high foreign prices, numerous enterprises exported most of
their output and thus caused shortages in the domestic
market place. Eventual cost savings were usually not
passed on to consumers in the form of lower prices,
but were absorbed through higher profits. Finally,
some enterprises reduced the output of basic neces-
sities whenever it seemed that they did not generate
satisfactory profits and, consequently, limited product choice and caused shortages in the domestic economy.

Limited Decentralization
of Authority

Simultaneously with the large-scale decentralization of economic decision-making authority to the
enterprise level, the reformers expected top managers
to delegate a substantial amount of authority, within
large industrial enterprises, from the head office
to individual units and, within individual units,
from the top to lower organizational levels. Such
comprehensive delegation of authority was expected
to increase organizational flexibility considerably
on both levels and, therefore, to improve over-all
industrial efficiency.

On both counts, the results of the first three
years were disappointing to the reformers.[33] In the
majority of large industrial enterprises, top managers in the head office continued to retain decision-
making authority in almost all major areas of activity. This maintained the complex and burdensome
relationships that made the efficient operation of
individual divisions so difficult during the pre-
reform years. Many marketing, profit-sharing, and
even personnel issues were decided at the head office and not by the divisional managers, who were
most intimately involved with the particular problems.

As could be expected, in the majority of industrial enterprises, such a high degree of authority
centralization strongly affected organizational structures, formal communication channels, and, most important, organizational flexibility and efficiency.
Spans of management in general were narrow, with
most top managers having only two or three subordinates reporting to them. Consequently, decisions
had to pass through several layers of management,
and authorizations were, more often than not, required by every individual manager. This resulted
in a slow decision-making process, causing unnecessary delays and occasional confusion.

Formal communication channels tended to be over-
loaded, with nonessential information flowing chiefly
from the lower to the higher echelons of management.
Consequently, in most industrial enterprises, the
atmosphere was characterized by a great deal of for-
mality. Middle-level managers, supporting administrative personnel, and, at times, even some top managers lacked initiative, showed little receptiveness
to change, and, thus, tended to follow rules and procedures in minute detail.

One of the most apparent results of the high
degree of centralization of authority was the involvement of the enterprise general managers and
their most immediate subordinates in matters that
deserved the attention of a reasonably able middle
manager at best. Top managers were swamped with
minute information concerning almost all types of
decisions and, consequently, could not possibly have
the time to discharge all their managerial functions
in a satisfactory manner.

The long-range planning function suffered most
of all, because top managers involved in short-term
operational decision-making could not spare the time
to evaluate and chart enterprise activities over the
next five to fifteen years. Furthermore, by retaining
most of the decision-making authority, top managers
made it almost impossible to improve the abilities
of their lower-level managers and, consequently, to
develop a systematic in-house management development

program that would prepare young and able subordinates
for vacant top managerial positions.

The reasons for the high degree of centralization of authority by top managers are complex. Historically, Hungarian society has always been more
authoritarian than democratic. The behavioral ves-
tiges of several centuries of feudalism can still be
detected in society at large, but, especially, among
those industrial workers who left their villages only
a few years before and were still not completely ac-
customed to the new industrial way of life. Unavoid-
ably, many middle and top managers also continued to
be influenced by what could best be described as the
historically conditioned authoritarian social atmosphere, and, consequently, developed and practiced an
authoritarian style of supervision.[34]

Although the central authorities strongly emphasized the need for a more-democratic style of
supervision and told the managers to encourage extensive employee participation in management activities, most top managers paid only lip service to the
idea and did not develop the needed organizational
prerequisites for such participation. Enterprise
committees composed of top managers, middle managers,
first-line supervisors, and workers were developed
in a rather pro forma manner and were never given a
real chance to emerge as an effective means of participation.

Information about enterprise operations in general and future plans in particular in most enterprises was not disseminated in a systematic and
comprehensive fashion among all employees. Many
managers seemed to believe that participation referred
to a kind of organizational arrangement that enabled
employees to get rid of frustrations and, on occasion, to tell off managers. Consequently, many
managers did not take the idea of employee participation too seriously.

In all fairness to the top managers, it has to
be pointed out that, in addition to their authoritarian tendencies, there were several other factors

that made the large-scale decentralization of authority more difficult than the reformers had believed
it would be. As mentioned before, there was a general shortage of well-qualified middle managers
throughout Hungarian industry. Consequently, a
large-scale decentralization of authority to middle
managers who lacked the necessary qualifications and
initiative and who were not used to organizational
power could have resulted in more organizational inefficiencies in the short run than the high degree
of centralization of authority had already caused.[35]
But, by not delegating authority and by not permit-
ting middle managers to learn through their own mistakes, the competence of lower-level managers could
hardly be improved, even in the long run.[36]

An additional factor limiting the decentralization of authority in the majority of industrial enterprises during 1968-70 was the need for top managers
to keep a careful check on the change-over of their
enterprise from an essentially passive organization
of the past to a more independent and active organization under NEM. Undoubtedly, during the initial
years, top managers probably had to be informed in
more detail about more activities than they probably
will be in the future. Nevertheless, the major factors causing the limited decentralization of authority were the generally authoritarian attitude of top
managers and the resulting style of supervision.
These are problems that the central authorities will
have to solve, especially as the educational level
and expectations of employees and workers increase
over the long run.

CONCLUDING REMARKS

The problems of NEM during 1968-70 were caused
by numerous interrelated factors, such as the lack of
a solid theoretical foundation, specific features of
the reform, and managerial attitudes and behavior.
Although, for discussion purposes, these problems
were classified as general, environmental, and managerial, their correction, from a practical point of
view, called for a simultaneously executed comprehensive set of changes and adjustments.

As pointed out several times before, the first
three years of the reform were marked by a careful
approach to change and to the correction of problems.
The reformers recognized the interrelated nature of
the problems and their causes and, since they did
not want to expose NEM to too many short-run dislocations, attempted to correct only those problems
where the solution was vital to the short-term functioning of NEM. All other changes and adjustments
were implemented in 1971 or were planned for the
1971-75 period.

NOTES

1. Oscar Lange pointed out, many years ago,
that Marxian economics does not provide enough operational concepts. See Oscar Lange, "Marxian Economics and Modern Economic Theory," in Marxism, ed. by
Michael Curtis (New York: Atherton Press, 1970),
pp. 215-18.

2. See Jenö Wilcsek, "Marketing a Szocialista
Gazdaságban" (Marketing in the Socialist Economy),
Figyelö, December 11, 1968, p. 3; László Szabó,
"Vállalati Üzletpolitika--Szocialista Marketing"
(Enterprise Policies--Socialist Marketing), Figyelö,
January 1, 1969, p. 6; Jenö Rédei, "Marketing a
Szocialista Gazdaságban" (Marketing in the Socialist
Economy), Figyelö, January 1, 1969, p. 6; Jenö Wilc-
sek, "Piackutatás és Szabályozott Piac" (Market Re-
search and the Regulated Market), Marketing-Piacku-
tatás, No. 4 (1968), pp. 7-12; Levente Fall, "A Gaz-
dasági Verseny és Marketing" (Economic Competition
and Marketing), Marketing-Piackutatás, No. 4 (1968),
pp. 32-39; and László Szabó, "A Piackutatás Aktuális
Problémái" (Current Problems of Market Research),
Marketing-Piackutatás, No. 1 (1971), pp. 5-12.

3. For a detailed discussion of these issues,
see Géza Peter Lauter, "The Changing Role of Marketing in the Eastern European Socialist Economies,"
Journal of Marketing, No. 4 (October, 1971), pp. 16-
20.

4. See Levente Fall, "A Gazdasági Verseny és Marketing" (Economic Competition and Marketing), Marketing-Piackutatás, No. 4 (1968), p. 36.

5. Jenö Wilcsek, "Piackutatás és Szabályozott Piac" (Market Research and the Regulated Market), Marketing-Piackutatás, No. 4 (1968), p. 11.

6. György Varga, "Távlati Tervezés a Magyar Vállalatoknál" (Long-Range Planning in Hungarian Enterprises), Közgazdasági Szemle (Economic Review), May, 1970, pp. 565-81.

7. Figyelö, April 8, 1970, p. 3.

8. Lajos Faluvégi, "A Szabályozási Rendszer és a Preferenciák" (The Regulatory System and Preferential Treatment), Gazdaság, March, 1971, pp. 7-21.

9. Magyar Statisztikai Zsebkönyv 1970 (Hungarian Statistical Pocketbook 1970) (Budapest: Központi Statisztikai Hivatal, 1971), p. 268.

10. See, for example, Béla Balassa, "The Economic Reform in Hungary," Economica, XXXIII (February, 1970), 6.

11. Figyelö, March 31, 1971, p. 5.

12. Népszabadság, February 22, 1968, p. 4.

13. Balassa, "The Economic Reform in Hungary," p. 8.

14. Tamás Nagy, "The Hungarian Economic Reform, Past and Future," Papers and Proceedings of the Eighty-Third Meeting (Menasha, Wis.: American Economic Association, May, 1971), p. 434.

15. György Kardos, "A Gazdasági Reform és Könyvkiadás" (The Economic Reform and Book Publishing), Kortars (The Contemporary) (1969), p. 1,102.

16. Figyelö, December 16, 1970, p. 4.

17.   Ibid., February 24, 1971, p. 2.

18.   Ibid., June 2, 1971, p. 1.

19.   Ibid., March 17, 1971, p. 3.

20.   Ibid., December 23, 1970, p. 4.

21.   Ibid., February 25, 1970, p. 3.

22.   Ibid., April 8, 1970, p. 5.

23.   Balassa, "The Economic Reform in Hungary,"
p. 16.

24.   Figyelö, March 11, 1970, p. 7.

25.   Ibid., January 20, 1971, p. 3.

26.   Ibid.

27.   Ibid., April 22, 1970, p. 4.

28.   Ibid.

29.   Ibid., April 8, 1970, p. 3.

30.   Lauter, "The Changing Role of Marketing,"
pp. 16-20.

31.   Karl Marx, Capital (Chicago: Charles H.
Kerr and Co., 1907), p. 169.

32.   Endre Megyeri, "Marketing Tapasztalatok a
Hazai Ipari, Bel és Külkereskedelmi Vállalatoknál"
(The Marketing Experiences of Domestic and Foreign-
Trade Industrial and Commercial Enterprises), Mar-
keting-Piackutatás, No. 1 (1970), pp. 5-9.

33.   Lajos Dózsa, ed., A Vállalati Belsö Mech-
anizmus Fejlesztésének Gyakorlati Kérdései (The
Practical Issues of the Further Development of the
Internal Enterprise Mechanism) (Budapest: A Magyar
Szocialista Munkáspárt Központi Bizottságának Gaz-
daságpolitikai Osztálya, 1971), pp. 10-14.

34.   For a detailed discussion of authoritarian versus participative styles of management, see Rensis Likert, The Human Organization: Its Management and Value (New York: McGraw-Hill, 1967).

35.   For empirical findings supporting this possibility, see Géza Peter Lauter, "Sociological, Cultural and Legal Factors Impeding Decentralization of Authority in Developing Countries," Academy of Management Journal, No. 3 (September, 1969), pp. 367-78.

36.   For an interesting discussion of the effects of participative management on productivity in Yugoslavia, see Arnold Tannenbaum et al., "Testing a Management Style," European Business, No. 27 (Autumn, 1970), pp. 60-68.

5

THE
FUTURE

Despite the numerous and complex problems discussed in Chapter 4, it became clear, by the end of
1970, that the reformers had successfully completed
the first, and probably the most difficult, phase
of transforming the Hungarian economy from a highly
centralized system into a more flexible, market-
oriented one. The over-all economic and social results were both promising: A more-balanced economic
growth pattern had been established, and the population had accepted NEM as an effective means of continually increasing the standard of living.

The year 1971 signaled the beginning of two
important developments. First, the Fourth Five-Year
Plan (1971-75) was started; and, second, the reformers
introduced a set of immediate changes and numerous
long-range, economic policy guidelines to alleviate
some of the problems of NEM. To avoid any conflicts,
both the changes and the new guidelines were coordi-
nated with the objectives of the new five-year plan.

As could be expected, the immediate changes were
developed chiefly to deal with the most pressing
problems caused by the managerial environment--that
is, by the various specific features of NEM. Both
the general structural problems and the managerial
problems--such as the limited role of profit as a
success indicator and the short-term outlook of most
industrial managers--were approached through a

combination of immediate changes and long-range guidelines, because their solution called for continuous
structural adjustments in the economy and behavioral
adjustments by the managers.

FOURTH FIVE-YEAR PLAN,
1971-75

The new five-year plan was developed within the
general planning structure established by NEM.
Throughout the entire planning process, the National
Planning Office stayed in touch with several advisory
committees, such as the Committee on Labor and the
Standard of Living and the Committee on Territorial
Development. Many of the issues and problems of the
plan were discussed in the public press and in professional journals. Consequently, for the first time
in more than two decades, the final plan was based on
a reasonable degree of consensus among the various
political, economic, and cultural groups, as well as
the more active, but unorganized, members of the
population.

The general guidelines of the new plan differ
from those of all previous plans in two important
respects. First, they call for an approximately equal
distribution of national income between new investments and consumption. Second, the previously neglected infrastructure, such as housing, is to receive
a much larger share of investment funds than ever before. Thus, it is clear that the central authorities
consider an increase in the standard of living over
the five-year plan period one of their most important
objectives.

More specifically, the new plan calls for an
average annual growth rate of 5.5-6.0 per cent.[1]
Total investments are to exceed new investments under
the Third Five-Year Plan (1966-70) by 30-32 per cent;
within this, industrial investments will be increased
23-25 per cent and infrastructure investments, 59-61
per cent. About 35 per cent of all industrial investments will be financed from the central budget; such
projects are designated to speed up technological

developments and the modernization of industrial
structures. The remaining 65 per cent of industrial
investments will be financed at the enterprise level.

Total industrial output is expected to go up 32-
34 per cent over the 1970 level, with the chemical
and construction industries in the lead. To accelerate technological development and to increase labor
productivity, approximately 2.5 per cent of national
income is budgeted for research and development. In
some industries, such as mining, ferrous metallurgy,
and food, however, the growth rate during 1971-75
will be below the average growth rate of past years.
Thus, in the new plan, the emphasis is no longer on
growth in all industrial branches at any cost.

Foreign-trade activities are expected to increase
30-40 per cent over the 1970 level. The general
guidelines of the plan call for more exports in engineering, light industry, and food products and for
higher imports of mining, metallurgical, and chemical
products, as well as electric power. Trade with the
socialist countries is to be increased 40-45 per cent
and with the nonsocialist (dollar-trade) countries,
33-35 per cent. In addition, the plan envisions more
cooperative agreements with both socialist and nonsocialist partners.

Annual price-level increases are limited to 1-2
per cent. The real per capita income of the population is scheduled to increase 25-27 per cent, and
consumption is expected to rise 29-30 per cent. The
increase in real income, however, will be accompanied
by a more-differentiated approach to income determination, whereby individual earnings will be based
chiefly upon skill and performance. Finally, the
plan envisions considerable improvements in the areas
of education, medicine, and culture.

CHANGES, GUIDELINES, AND
IMPROVEMENTS, 1971

The changes introduced as of January 1, 1971,
and throughout the year were designed chiefly to

modify specific features of NEM and, thus, the managerial environment.[2] They consisted mostly of new rules and regulations and, consequently, were implemented through government decrees. It would, however, be a mistake to assume that the decrees were issued in the same heavy-handed manner as during the pre-reform years. On the contrary, they were based on an evaluation of experiences during the first three years of NEM, as well as on detailed political, economic, and social studies performed by the various government, academic, and social institutions.

The new economic policy guidelines were, in most cases, included in the new five-year-plan, in the interpretations of the new rules and regulations, and in other official publications. These guidelines expressed the long-range economic policy intentions of the central authorities and recommended, in a general way, courses of action that would enable managers to conform to the expectations of the central authorities and the objectives of the Fourth Five-Year Plan.

System of Competition

As pointed out in Chapter 4, the general lack of effective competition in most sectors of the Hungarian economy was a major problem that interfered with the proper functioning of NEM. In recognizing that effective over-all competition would be a long-range development involving major structural changes in the economy, the reformers focused on improvements in capital movements as a start in that direction.

To this end, the rules governing the formation of enterprise associations were changed. Although the 1968 version of NEM permitted the formation of enterprise associations, it did not authorize enterprises to obtain capital from one another. Consequently, during 1968-70, only a limited number of enterprise associations were formed, none of which contributed to the improvement of competitive conditions. Therefore, according to a new rule, enterprise associations are no longer differentiated on the basis of ownership but on the basis of the nature of the relationship between the participating

enterprises.[3] Enterprises can now form either a
"simple association" or a "common enterprise."

A simple association is based on cooperative
working agreements, such as cooperative advertising,
purchasing, and selling. Such cooperative activities
can be financed from the unobligated portions of
enterprise development funds and from the unobligated
portions of variable (working) and fixed capital.
The simple association does not represent a legal
entity, and each participating enterprise, therefore,
continues to meet all of its obligations toward the
state, such as tax payments, on an individual basis.
If so desired, however, the simple association can
adopt a common name.

The common enterprise is based on a permanent
and close relationship between the participating
enterprises. Its creation requires the permission
of the respective industrial branch minister and the
agreement of the Minister of Finance. (Foreign partners can also participate with the permission of the
Minister of Finance.) A common enterprise is a legal
entity and is managed by a board of directors composed
of the representative of each participating enterprise. As in the case of a simple association, the
financing of a common enterprise can be done from
unobligated portions of enterprise development funds
and from the unobligated portions of variable (working) and fixed capital.

Invested capital becomes the property of the
common enterprise, and, although a common enterprise
can generate its own development fund, participating
enterprises can transfer part of their profit-sharing
fund (if it is sufficiently large) to the common
development fund. Without limitation, a part of their
development fund can also be transferred. Profits
can be withdrawn by the participating enterprises on
the basis of a mutually agreed-upon legal contract
through which, if they so desire, enterprises can
also transfer other rights and obligations to the
common enterprise. Although individual profit shares
are not regulated by the state, not more than 50 per
cent of commonly earned profits can be withdrawn by
the participating enterprises together.

As a legal entity, the common enterprise has to meet all obligations toward the state in the same manner as does a single enterprise. Eventual losses have to be covered from the common reserve fund, but, if it is not sufficiently large, individual enterprises can make contributions to it from their own reserve funds. If a common enterprise is dissolved, all obligations toward third parties have to be met by the participating enterprises; their individual financial liability, however, is limited to the extent of their investment.

In addition to capital transfers through enterprise associations, the new rules also authorize individual enterprises to transfer, temporarily or permanently, unobligated development funds or equipment to one another with or without charge, but only for development purposes. The charge can take the form of interest payments or leasing fees. To assure maximum flexibility, no supervisory agency has the authority to interfere with such arrangements unless they involve illegal activities.

The reformers are confident that, within a reasonable period of time, numerous industrial enterprises will take advantage of the new rules and that, consequently, competitive conditions will gradually improve in most industries. Such expectations are probably justified. It must be pointed out, however, that the new rules in themselves can be considered only a good starting point. For industrial enterprises to exploit the available opportunities fully and, thus, to engage in large-scale capital transfers, the short-term outlook of managers and their general unwillingness to take risks must also change. The formation of associations, especially of common enterprises, and the use of the various other means of capital movements call for good long-range planning, intelligent risk-taking, and a considerable amount of tolerance toward uncertainty--managerial qualities that are currently in short supply in most industrial enterprises.

Role of Profit

As was noted above, the role of profit as a success indicator was rather limited in most enterprises during 1968-70. The officially determined scheme of allocating profit among the various enterprise funds was complex and rigid and tended to make it less expensive for managers to employ additional labor than to invest in labor-saving equipment when expanding operations. Furthermore, the various direct and indirect subsidies--such as export subsidies, tax concessions, and direct financial grants--considerably improved the profit position of numerous inefficient enterprises.

As could be expected, this made the efficient allocation of economic resources difficult. Consequently, attempts to improve productivity and to introduce technical inventions were also negatively affected. Finally, the rather inconsistent subsidy policies of the central authorities reintroduced the possibility of bargaining between industrial managers and the authorities. To overcome these problems, at least partially, the central authorities changed the rules governing the distribution of profit among the various enterprise funds, limited the burden put on the development fund, and revised the policies concerning subsidies.

In the computation of enterprise profit, the labor-cost multiplication factor has been increased from 2 to 3. In other words, the cost of labor, as opposed to the cost of new equipment, is increased. Furthermore, the profit-sharing fund is now taxed progressively at rates between 40 per cent and 70 per cent and not at rates between 0 per cent and 70 per cent, as in the past. Table 27 presents the new tax rates applied to the profit-sharing fund as of January 1, 1971. As a consequence of the new tax schedule, the average tax rate on most enterprise profit-sharing funds increases to approximately 60 per cent. This increase is expected to narrow the difference between the tax burden of the profit-sharing fund and the development fund, as well as between the profit-sharing funds of various enterprises.

TABLE 27

Profit-Sharing Fund Tax Rates, 1971

Profit-Sharing Fund (as per cent of wages)	Tax Rate (per cent)
0-6	40
6-12	50
12-20	60
20 and over	70

Source: Otto Gadó, ed., Közgazdasági Szabal-yozó Rendszerünk Továbbfejlesztése (The Continued Development of Our Economic Regulatory System) (Budapest: Közgazdasági és Jogi Könyvkiadó, 1970), p. 57.

The enterprise development funds continue to be subjected to a 60-per-cent straight tax, on the average. To overcome the reduction in enterprise development funds caused by the increased labor-cost multiplication factor, management is authorized to transfer money from the profit-sharing fund to the development fund. To promote such transfer, the tax on the amount involved is only two-thirds of the tax applicable to the development fund. Furthermore, to reduce the burden on the development fund, the previously applicable communal tax (2 per cent of annual wages) that had to be paid out of the development fund was eliminated and replaced by a 6-per-cent community contribution to be paid out of total profits earned. The various insurance payments also no longer have to be charged against the development fund.

Enterprise reserve funds continually have to be at the level where they equal 8 per cent of the annual wage bill plus 1.5 per cent of the gross value of fixed and variable assets (capital). If, however, this amount is less than 80 per cent of the sum of

the 1971 profit-based maximum profit-sharing and development funds, the required level of the reserve
fund is the latter amount. Furthermore, the annual
contribution of the profit-sharing and development
funds to the reserve fund was raised from 10 per cent
to 12.5 per cent. These new rules, in general, were
designed to promote a more even development of reserve
funds throughout the economy and to equalize the burden associated with the creation of such funds among
the various enterprises.

     According to the new guidelines, the subsidy
policies of the central authorities are based more
on the economic issues involved in a particular situation than on other, economically unjustifiable considerations, such as political issues. Whenever
possible, subsidies are allocated on a competitive
basis and, preferably, only to enterprises in growth
industries. The central authorities also decided to
prevent inefficient enterprises from creating a development fund out of subsidies, thus making it very
difficult for such enterprises to expand operations.

     In addition to the general subsidy guidelines,
the central authorities introduced a new set of
specific rules concerning export subsidies. According
to the new rules, as of January 1, 1971, enterprises
engaged in foreign trade receive export subsidies on
a branch, rather than an individual, basis, as in the
past. (The branches are determined on the basis of
the substitutability of products exported. They do
not, however, represent industries.) The new branch
export subsidies are a function of the regular foreign-trade price multiplier, to which a special
branch subsidy factor is added by the central authorities. Under such conditions, the foreign-currency
earnings of an enterprise are multiplied by the new
branch multiplier, and enterprises in the same branch
receive the same domestic-currency earnings per unit
of export.

     Although the central authorities intended to
avoid granting export subsidies to individual enterprises, the differences in efficiency among enterprises in the same branch called for some individual

considerations. To this end, enterprises engaged in
foreign trade are classified in two major groups:
those that do not receive any export subsidies and
that are, therefore, entitled to tax concessions and
those that receive export subsidies. Enterprises in
the latter group are further classified according to
their relationship to the officially determined
branch multiplier.

Enterprises for which the per unit cost of export
is between the official foreign-trade price multiplier
and the branch multiplier receive export price subsidies in accordance with the branch multiplier.
Thus, the more efficient an enterprise is, the more
export subsidies it can receive over and above the
amount it requires. This increases enterprise profit
and, consequently, enlarges the profit-sharing and
development funds. This feature of the new subsidy
system is designed to promote enterprise efficiency.

Enterprises for which the per unit cost of export is higher than the branch multiplier receive
subsidies on the basis of individual considerations.
If, for example, the per unit cost of export of such
an enterprise is relatively close to the branch multiplier, it can receive a regressive export subsidy that
will be terminated by the end of 1975. If, however,
the per unit cost of export of an enterprise is considerably higher than the branch multiplier, it can
receive, if absolutely necessary, a subsidy to enlarge
its profit-sharing funds but not its development fund.

Although the changes and guidelines introduced
in 1971 have somewhat improved the role of profit as
an enterprise success indicator, it is clear that much
more has to be done before enterprise profit can truly
fulfill its role as an efficient allocator of economic
resources. Most of all, the still-artificial producer
and consumer price systems have to be reformed to reflect true scarcity values. Unless this is done at
some point in time, the current, and any future,
changes in the rules and guidelines concerning enterprise profit can be considered as only an attempt to
treat the symptoms, rather than the causes, of the
problems.

Material-Supply System

Despite the considerable flexibility introduced into the material-supply system during the first three years of NEM, it became apparent, by 1970, that the reformed supply system did not meet the expectations of the central authorities and the industrial managers. Channels of distribution continued to be slow and rigid, alternative channels were rarely available, delivery dates were not always kept, and, consequently, occasional supply shortages tended to disrupt industrial production. Changes and guidelines introduced during 1971 will, for the most part, become effective over time; thus, no immediate improvements can be expected.

To shorten and simplify channels of distribution, the central authorities decided to curtail the activities of selected trading enterprises and to grant independent import licenses to more industrial and commercial enterprises. Several trading enterprises were instructed to develop a distribution system serving small and medium-sized buyers; the funds necessary for the development of such a system are guaranteed by the central authorities. In general, the central authorities decided to support financially, if necessary, the reorganization of any distribution channel for the sake of improvement. Finally, trading enterprises received the authority to rent any warehousing facility to industrial and commercial enterprises, even if it is the only service that an industrial or commercial enterprise wishes.

As for the guidelines, the central authorities decided to continue, over the next few years, the gradual elimination of supply trade limitations whenever possible. Such limitations will be retained only if the desired material balances cannot be established through the various economic regulators, such as prices, taxes, and credit. Compulsory delivery contracts, for example, will be applied only if national defense and health interests require their use. Minimum inventory requirements will also be applied only in exceptional cases.

Considering the nature and seriousness of the
supply problems, the changes and guidelines introduced
in 1971 appear to be rather limited. In most cases,
the central authorities instructed and informed the
trading enterprises about the kinds of changes to be
made and the type of guidelines that will affect the
material-supply system in the years to come. It
seems, however, that, as with the limited role of
profit as a success indicator, the over-all conditions
in the material-supply system can be improved only
through a reform of the producer price system. Furthermore, it appears that a transformation of the
time-consuming and rigid channels of distribution into
shorter and more flexible ones calls not only for the
availability of needed funds but also for a far more
forward-looking, risk-taking attitude on the part of
trading enterprise managers. The 1971 changes and
new guidelines, however, do little in this respect.

Price System

As mentioned previously, the artificial nature
of the domestic price system represents one of the
most difficult problems that the Hungarian reformers
have to cope with. Domestic consumer and producer
prices deviate from each other and, in general, do
not reflect true scarcity values. Furthermore, domestic consumer and producer prices deviate considerably from foreign prices; consequently, the increased
participation of Hungary in the international division
of labor is impeded.

Although the central authorities recognized both
the importance and the magnitude of the problem, they
continued to refrain from fundamentally revising the
price system primarily for two reasons. First, the
artificially low level of certain consumer, and even
producer, prices was desirable from a sociopolitical
point of view. Second, a fundamental revision of the
domestic price system could take place only over a
long period of time. Too many immediate changes would
seriously upset the existing economic relationships
(however artificial) and, thus, conceivably cause more
harm in the short run than had the currently used
price system.

Based on these considerations, the 1971 changes and guidelines were of a rather limited nature, with both producer and consumer price structures remaining essentially intact. Only housing rents underwent a substantial revision on July 1, 1971. Prior to this date, rents covered only about 35-40 per cent of the maintenance costs of all state-owned housing. Annual government housing subsidies, consequently, amounted to approximately 2 billion forint.[4]

According to the new rules, rent now has to cover all maintenance expenses. Depreciation charges and the cost of capital invested in building, however, are not included in the new rent payments; these costs are charged against the central budget. To overcome the resulting financial burden on many families caused by increased rents, the central authorities also decided to grant, for a limited number of years, a housing allowance based on total family income. After early 1972, such allowances will be gradually reduced whenever possible.

To eliminate some of the problems caused by deviations between domestic and foreign prices, the central authorities announced that, starting in 1971, the Minister of Finance, together with other concerned agencies, can require or permit enterprises engaged in foreign trade to generate an import or export price-differential reserve fund. Although the new funds, in general, will complement the existing enterprise reserve fund, they are specifically designed to reduce the burden on the central budget and on the central authorities, who, in the past, frequently had to adjust the various financial regulators whenever foreign prices fluctuated in the short run. (A permanent surplus or deficit of the new funds, for example, indicates permanent foreign price changes.)

The import price-differential reserve fund is applicable chiefly to enterprises importing basic materials or semimanufactured goods with domestically controlled prices, but with strongly fluctuating foreign prices. (Importers of products for which domestic prices are free can be instructed or permitted to develop such a fund if over-all economic considerations necessitate its development. The same

applies to enterprises for which imports normally do
not generate excess earnings.) The source of the
fund is the excess earnings that result from the difference between the officially set domestic base price
and the given import price. The funds thus generated
have to be deposited in the National Bank, and the
rules governing their disposition are centrally determined.

The export price-differential reserve fund can
be required of, or granted to, industrial enterprises
that export products in large quantities to those
nonsocialist (dollar-trade) markets where price
changes last for longer periods of time. (If specialized foreign-trade commercial enterprises export
such products on their own account, they can also
generate such a fund.) The fund is generated by the
difference between the given base price of a product
and the excess earnings obtained through foreign
price increases. Such excess earnings have to be
separated from the regular earnings of the enterprises and deposited in the reserve fund (on account
with the National Bank), which, if and when foreign
prices decrease, can be used to cover the resulting
losses.

With respect to the general price guidelines,
the central authorities made it clear that no substantial changes are planned in the producer and
consumer price system for the 1971-75 period. They
emphasized that, although the development of a more-
effective price system is still an important long-
range objective, the number of producer and consumer
prices still controlled--as well as their general
level--cannot be changed significantly over the next
few years. Attempts will be made, however, to stop
the persistent price increases of major investment
goods, such as machines. Imports of such products
will be increased, and managers will continually be
advised to develop more-flexible and market-oriented
price strategies whenever possible and, most important
to pass on cost savings to consumers in the form of
lower prices.

The 1971 changes in the Hungarian price system thus failed to introduce any substantial modifications in the essentially artificial domestic and foreign price relationships. Because the price policy guidelines for 1971-75 did not indicate any important adjustments either, it is apparent that the reformers believed that it is too early to expose NEM to the undoubtedly severe shocks that could result from a short-term transformation of the existing price system into a more efficient one.

Investment and Credit System

In addition to the artificial price structures, the investment and credit system of NEM proved to be one of the weakest links in the new economic order. As discussed previously, the over-all economic efficiency of most new investments was not satisfactory; as a consequence of the financial rules and competitive conditions, inefficient enterprises expanded, whereas enterprises in growth industries could not obtain the needed funds. Numerous new projects were not properly evaluated, and planned cost overruns were frequent; the resulting shortage of funds, therefore, forced managers to leave many new investments unfinished. Capital, in general, was scarce, and the prices of most investment goods tended to be high.

To improve the situation, the central authorities introduced several changes. Industrial enterprises with fixed assets having a short life expectancy and a relatively low value can now receive back part or all of the 40 per cent of total depreciation charges that, in the past, were retained by the central authorities for the central budget. This is expected to supplement the development funds and, thus, to enable enterprises possessing such assets to replace the same in a more-continuous fashion.

To promote investments in priority areas, the central authorities decided to offer, on a competitive-bidding basis, development fund tax concessions to enterprises that are willing to undertake investment projects listed in the central plan. The bidding conditions are published jointly by the National Planning Office, the Ministry of Finance, and the concerned branch ministry. Such conditions include detailed descriptions of the investment project, its expected results, foreign-trade consequences, the nature of related investments, and, occasionally, a specification of the type of enterprise that may participate in the bidding.

When submitting cost estimates, participating enterprises must specify, among other factors, the fixed and variable portions of capital to be used, the ruble and dollar costs of needed imports, the size of the development fund, and the amount of credit needed. If the enterprise winning the bidding fails to complete the investment project, the tax concessions are withdrawn and the already obtained funds have to be repaid to the central authorities.

As of January 1, 1971, state loans granted to enterprises for investment projects are also allocated on a competitive-bidding basis. The purpose of such loans is to enable enterprises to undertake desirable investments listed in the central plan, even though they do not possess the needed funds. The loans are granted at a lower interest rate and for longer pe- riods of time than are Investment Bank loans. State grants to enterprises for investment are made only under special circumstances, such as when investment projects listed in the central plan are not under- taken by any enterprise because of a lack of funds, unfavorable prices, or other managerially uncontrol- lable factors.

Funds from such grants can be used only for the stated purpose, and any enterprise that fails to do so has to return the entire amount, together with an appropriate interest-rate penalty. Finally, if an enterprise is willing to undertake two different in- vestment projects, but, because of the central plan priorities, one project has to be preferred over the other, the central authorities, to support the enter- prise, may take over the bank loan interest-rate pay- ments.

To improve the functioning of the credit system, the central authorities on January 1, 1971, provided much-needed variable (working) capital to those enterprises that had not received such capital at the start of NEM. All enterprises were also authorized to lend unobligated funds to one another, to provide credit on sales, and to offer or to accept advance payments on future sales. The meeting of the variable (working) capital needs of all enterprises and the increased flexibility in interenterprise financial relationships made it possible for the central authorities to define clearly the nature and use of the various types of bank loans available to enterprises.

According to the new definitions, as of 1971, the banks are authorized to grant short-term loans (maximum, 24 months) to help enterprises overcome temporary capital shortages. Such loans can be given on the basis of the creditworthiness of the applicant alone. Medium-term loans can be granted for up to 60 months on a competitive basis, but only for well-defined investment projects. Applications for such loans have to be accompanied by detailed economic studies of the proposed project. Long-term loans (maximum, 12 years) can be given on a competitive basis to help finance preferred investment projects listed in the annual credit directives. Such loans can be granted at a considerably lower interest rate than can the short- and medium-term loans.

As for the general investment and credit guidelines, the central authorities announced that, over the 1971-75 period, investments in the public transportation, natural gas, aluminum, data-processing, and textile industries will be on the preferred list. Although numerous projects will be financed from the central budget, the number of centrally determined and financed investment projects is supposed to decline gradually over the next few years. By 1975, for example, only about 28 per cent of all industrial investments will be centrally determined; the remaining 72 per cent will be undertaken and financed at the enterprise level.[5]

The investment and credit system changes and guidelines introduced during 1971, thus, were rather modest. Undoubtedly, the central authorities have tried to improve the economic efficiency of investments and to reduce tension in the investment-goods and capital markets; however, hamstrung by numerous previous investment commitments, the artificial price system, artificial interest rates, and the unsatisfactory planning and management of new investment projects at the enterprise level, they could not, in the short run, significantly improve the situation. As in the case of the price system, fundamental improvements in the investment and credit system can take place only in the long run.

Employment, Labor Relations, and Incentive System

According to the Fourth Five-Year Plan, improved labor productivity should account for 80 per cent of the 1971-75 increase in national income generated by the industrial sector of the economy. In light of the labor-productivity problems discussed in Chapter 4, the accomplishment of this objective is a demanding task. To increase labor productivity significantly, the central authorities introduced several important changes dealing with employment, labor relations, and the incentive system.

In computing taxable profits, enterprises can now report as costs all average annual wage increases. Consequently, average annual wage increases no longer have to be deducted from the profit-sharing fund. Any enterprise that raises average annual wages has to pay a one-time, special tax on such a raise from the profit-sharing fund. The size of this tax is a function of the relationship between the annual percentage increase of average wages and an enterprise efficiency index defined as the sum of annual wages and profit, divided by the number of employees.

A 1-per-cent increase in this index entitles management to increase average wages by 0.3 per cent; this amount is taxed at 50 per cent of the increase. Average annual wage increases exceeding the 0.3-per-

cent maximum are taxed in a steeply progressive manner. Starting in 1972, the computation of annual
wage increases has to be based on the average wage
level of the previous year. (Because of transitional
difficulties, the 1971 average wage increases were
computed on a different basis.) The essence of this
change is that, under the new rule, management can
increase average wages only if it minimizes the number of employees.

On July 1, 1971, the industrial wage and salary
classification system was modified, and the income
of approximately 400,000 nonindustrial employees,
such as teachers and military officers, was raised.[6]
The new industrial wage and salary classification
system is based on the premise that only a highly
differentiated wage and salary system, taking into
account education, experience, and performance, can
serve as an effective financial motivator.

The new system specifies only the upper and lower
wage and salary limits; individual earnings have to
be determined by management and the labor unions
through collective-bargaining agreements by January
1, 1973. Table 28 presents the new managerial salary
classification system, which includes all top managers, their immediate deputies, and the heads of large
departments and their deputies. Table 29 presents
the new salary classification system for supporting
administrative personnel.

Effective July 22, 1971, the central authorities
also decided to limit moonlighting in general and
part-time employment in particular. According to the
new rules, employees must have written permission
from their full-time employer before they can accept
an additional job. If the additional job interferes
with the effective performance of the full-time job,
management is required to deny permission. Furthermore, any part-time employment has to be recorded in
the employee's workbook.

Although the 1970 revisions of the incentive
system considerably improved the effectiveness of the
profit-sharing plan as a financial motivator, the

TABLE 28

Managerial Salary Classification System (on Monthly Basis)
(Forint)[a]

Managerial Position	Enterprise Category[b]					
	Special	A	B	C	D
General manager	6,500-8,000	5,500-7,200	4,700-6,400	4,000-5,700	3,500-5,200
Deputy general manager	5,500-6,000	4,700-6,400	4,000-5,700	3,500-5,200	3,200-4,800
Major department head	3,900-6,000	3,600-5,500	3,300-5,200	3,100-4,800	3,000-4,400
Deputy department head	3,200-5,000	3,200-5,000	3,000-4,600	2,900-4,300	2,700-4,000

[a]At official exchange rate of 30 forint to U.S. $1.
[b]Based on economic significance and size.

Source: Figyelö, April 21, 1971, p. 2.

TABLE 29

Supporting Administrative Personnel Salary Classification System (on Monthly Basis) (Forint)[a]

Years of Experience or Special Qualifications	Educational Qualification Category[b]			
	I	II	III	IV
0-3	1,000-1,900	1,300-2,200	1,600-2,600	1,900-3,000
3-8	1,300-2,200	1,600-2,600	1,900-3,000	2,200-3,300
8-15	1,600-2,600	1,900-3,000	2,200-3,300	2,500-3,600
15-20	1,900-3,000	2,200-3,300	2,500-3,600	2,800-4,000
20 and over	2,200-3,300	2,500-3,600	2,800-4,000	3,100-4,400
Technical and economic consultants			4,000-5,000	4,400-6,000

[a]At official exchange rate of 30 forint to U.S. $1.
[b]Category I includes all those who do not qualify for other categories, which range from high school graduates (Category II) to university graduates (Category IV).

Source: Figyelö, April 21, 1971, p. 2.

165

central authorities introduced some additional changes
to the system during 1971. These changes were designed to promote the transformation of the short-
term managerial outlook into a more forward-looking
one. The nature of these changes, however, is such
that, currently, they can be applied only to those
industrial enterprises that have well-defined, me-
dium-range objectives for which accomplishment can
be reasonably well measured. In other words, the
changes apply chiefly to those large enterprises
that are working toward the accomplishment of centrally determined objectives.

In managing the incentive system for top managers of such enterprises, the supervisory authorities,
such as the branch ministries, can withhold up to 25
per cent of the annually due profit shares. If the
centrally determined objectives are accomplished in
an efficient manner within three to five years, the
supervisory authorities are expected to repay the
accumulated sum to top managers. If the objectives
are accomplished in an exceptional manner, the supervisory authorities can pay additional bonuses from
the enterprise wage fund.

General guidelines affecting employment, labor
relations, and the incentive system dealt chiefly
with the need for development of a highly differentiated and effective financial motivation system.
Managers were told to review carefully and to revise
enterprise wage and salary structures along the lines
of the new wage and salary classification system.
Furthermore, they were told to discontinue their
egalitarian approach to wage, salary, and profit-
share determinations and to reward individual employees on the basis of education, experience, and performance.

The 1971 changes and guidelines, together with
the 1970 changes, provided industrial enterprise
managers with a far more flexible motivational system
than the one used during 1968-70. The central authorities have apparently done almost everything
possible to enable managers to increase labor productivity through the skillful application of financial

motivators at the enterprise level. The only ques-
tion that remains is whether industrial managers have
the skill and the courage to utilize the new system
effectively during the 1971-75 period.

Foreign-Trade System

As explained in Chapter 4, attempts of the reformers to increase the participation of Hungary in
the international division of labor and economic cooperation were impeded by several factors. The major
problems were deviations between domestic and foreign
prices, the high cost of numerous imports from nonsocialist countries, COMECON trade agreements and
price relationships, the limited use of close cooperative agreements between domestic foreign-trade
and industrial enterprises, and the reluctance of
enterprise managers to take full advantage of the international capital markets.

As could be expected, the 1971 changes in the
foreign-trade system were limited by the artificial
nature of the domestic price system and, thus, could
not lead to an elimination of most of the problems.
Undoubtedly, the creation of the export and import
price-differential funds reduced the heavy burden on
the central authorities, who no longer have to adjust
the various financial regulators whenever a temporary
price change occurs in the foreign markets. The
changes in export subsidy policies have also considerably reduced the burden on the central budget, and
the granting of subsidies on a branch basis may succeed in promoting the expansion of efficient export-
ing enterprises and in limiting the growth of enterprises with inefficient foreign-trade activities.

To promote technological improvements throughout
Hungarian industry and to ease tension in domestic
investment-goods markets, the central authorities
also decided to decrease tariffs on imported machines
and technical equipment during 1971. Furthermore,
to lower the prices of selected imported consumer
goods and to improve consumer product choice, tariffs
and taxes on many items were reduced.

In addition to the domestic developments, the
agreement by the COMECON countries on a long-range
integration plan (at their Twenty-Fifth Session in
Bucharest, Romania, on July 27-29, 1971) was another
notable event that affected Hungary's foreign-trade
relations. According to the agreement, the number
of COMECON consultative meetings will increase in
the future, and efforts will be made to improve the
coordination of national plans in terms of specific
details, such as investment, research and development, and financial programs. Great emphasis was
put on the need for better coordination between the
product-specialization objectives of the chemical
and machine industries.

The agreement did not call for significant
changes in COMECON trade relationships. Although the
number of quotas used may decrease, trade relationships will continue to be based on long-range bilateral agreements. The agreement also calls for continued detailed price studies and sets 1980 as the
year in which a decision concerning realistic exchange rates and the role of the transfer ruble has
to be reached. Finally, to accomplish all of these
objectives, the agreement specifies the creation of
an International Investment Bank, a Committee for
Planning Cooperation, and a Committee for Scientific
and Technical Cooperation, as well as other agencies,
as important short-range objectives.

The foreign-trade guidelines for 1971-75 continue to be based on the need for close cooperation
with the COMECON countries. Ruble trade is expected
to increase 45-50 per cent over the 1970 level; dollar trade, 33-35 per cent. Long-range bilateral
agreements with the Soviet Union, the German Democratic Republic, Czechoslovakia, Bulgaria, Poland,
Romania, and Yugoslavia have already been signed.

Numerous trade agreements were also closed with
nonsocialist countries in 1971. Most of these agreements, however, are of a somewhat shorter duration;
the longest ones run out in 1974. In establishing
trade relationships with the nonsocialist world, the
central authorities put great emphasis on the need

to improve considerably the technology of Hungarian
industry through the increased purchase of licenses
and more cooperative agreements with individual firms.
(The per capita expenditure on licensing agreements
in Hungary is among the lowest in Europe.)

The 1971 changes and guidelines affecting the
foreign-trade system, thus, did not result in a fundamental improvement of Hungary's foreign-trade relationships. As mentioned several times before, the
artificial domestic price system and the resulting
deviations of foreign prices from domestic prices
have not been changed, and, consequently, no over-all
improvements have been possible. Although the COMECON
integration plan may some day result in more-realistic
trade relationships between the member countries,
the 1971 agreement did not considerably change the
existing trade system. Long-range bilateral agreements, nonconvertible currencies, a limited transfer
ruble, and unrealistic price relationships will probably continue to plague all member countries, but
expecially Hungary, for years to come.

REMAINING PROBLEMS

The 1971 changes introduced by the central authorities were designed to eliminate, or at least
reduce, simultaneously many of the problems that
emerged during the first three years of NEM. As
pointed out above, in some cases, the changes seemed
to promise considerable improvements; in other cases,
however, it appeared that they did not go far enough,
and, consequently, no beneficial developments can be
expected.

In addition to the rather limited nature of many
1971 changes, the central authorities also appeared
to have neglected the correction of several problems.
Undoubtedly, as a result of time pressure, limited
resources, the vital significance of some problems,
and other related factors, priority decisions had to
be made. This does not, however, mean that the neglected problems can continually be ignored without
endangering the long-range future of NEM.

Several of the remaining problems will probably be corrected by the passage of time and through the increased experience of the central authorities and managers with the functioning of a competitively oriented socialist economic system. The problems of a limited theoretical foundation, the lack of satisfactory planning information, and managerial independence fall into this category. Others, however, such as the irregular production pattern, inadequate managerial planning and risk-taking, the limited decentralization of authority, and the inadequate performance of marketing at the enterprise level, call for a systematic and comprehensive managerial education effort on the part of the central authorities.

The major causes of all of these problems--the short-term outlook and the rather authoritarian attitudes of most managers--are behavioral factors that are very difficult to change. The problem is further compounded by the strong possibility that Hungarian industrial managers, to improve labor discipline in the short run, are now going to behave in an even more authoritarian manner than they did before. Finally, the central authorities also have to see to it that, through widespread training programs, more-qualified middle managers and staff specialists can be employed by industrial enterprises, because, otherwise, the currently somewhat slow and burdensome decision-making process cannot be improved.

CONVERGENCE OR DIVERGENCE?

Ever since the economic systems of the Western capitalist and the Eastern European socialist countries started undergoing fundamental changes, since the 1950's, interested observers have been speculating about the long-range implications of such developments. The increased influence of government in economic life and the application of some form of central planning in numerous capitalist countries, on the one hand, and the experiments with forms of market organization and large-scale economic decentralization in the socialist countries, on the other hand, have prompted scholars like Tinbergen, Rostow, and Galbraith to argue that both systems have started on the road to convergence.[7] As Galbraith put it,

> Such reflection on the future would also emphasize the convergent tendencies of industrial societies, however different their popular or ideological billing; the convergence being to a roughly similar design for organization and planning. . . . Convergence begins with modern large-scale production, with heavy requirements of capital, sophisticated technology and, as a prime consequence, elaborate organization. . . .
>
> Thus convergence between the two ostensibly different industrial systems occurs at all fundamental points.[8]

The essence of such arguments is that the commonality of science and technology tends, at certain stages of economic development, to produce similar industrial complexes, techniques of analysis, managerial practices, patterns of behavior, and, thus, similar socioeconomic organizations and administration. Such solutions to industrial problems, whenever believed to be useful, are freely borrowed from each other. The borrowing of these solutions, in turn, continually reinforces the converging development tendencies of both systems, and this, in the long run, could result in the emergence of a new socioeconomic and managerial system comprised of the best of both worlds.

The introduction of NEM appears to support the arguments of the convergence theorists. The fundamental reorganization of the Hungarian economy has indeed resulted in the implementation of capitalist economic and managerial concepts, as well as the large-scale borrowing of economic and managerial experiences from both the capitalist and the socialist worlds. As pointed out in Chapter 4, such developments were necessitated by the limited theoretical foundations of the reform and by the need to develop new concepts within a relatively short period of time.

The emergence of managers as the new social elite
and the increased emphasis on standardized mass production and mass marketing of consumer goods to increase the standard of living also seem to reinforce
the validity of the convergence theory.

Undoubtedly, there is an element of truth in
all of these observations and, consequently, in the
convergence theory as applied to Hungary. It would
be an oversimplification, however, to argue, therefore, that, on the socialist side, Hungary, together
with Yugoslavia, is leading the way toward the ultimate merging of the socialist and the capitalist
economic systems. Nothing of that sort is happening.
NEM is the answer of an intelligent and energetic
people to the many questions raised by a rigid and
burdensome economic system of the past.

The main features of NEM are based on an un-
questioned allegiance of the reformers to Marxian
political and economic ideology; they are shaped by
the realities of present-day power politics and by
the deep-rooted cultural legacy of a proud nation.
In this sense, NEM is different from any of the other
reforms in the Eastern European socialist economies
and quite unlike any of the gradually changing capitalist economies.

The cultural differences are especially important in this respect. Experience shows that attitudes toward life and acceptable behavior patterns
are slow to change, even under the pressures of uni-
fying economic developments. It is probably reasonable to argue that long-established attitudes and
behavior patterns will change only to the extent
that enables a society to absorb the major elements
of new technology, industrial organization, and managerial techniques.

It is, of course, impossible to predict what
will happen in the long run. The possibility of unexpected political and even economic developments
cannot be ruled out. On the basis of this study,
however, it seems reasonable to argue that, although
NEM is an important development in the socialist

world, it is by no means conclusive evidence in support of the convergence theory. It appears, rather,
that NEM validates the idea of parallel, but still
differing, economic and managerial developments in
both the Eastern European socialist and the Western
capitalist countries. In other words, although there
tend to be points of similarity in both economic and
managerial systems, these similarities do not imply
that divergent points or changes are absent or are
of lesser importance.

CONCLUDING REMARKS

The objectives of the Fourth Five-Year Plan and
the changes, as well as the guidelines, introduced
during 1971 are evidence that Hungary's NEM is here
to stay. Both the government and the population appear to be committed to the new industrialization
strategy. Although many of the 1971 changes did not
go far enough and, thus, could not eliminate or even
minimize many of the major problems, it is clear that
the central authorities are only waiting for a more
opportune time to modify and improve NEM additionally.
On the whole, the reform appears to be a successful
attempt to increase the efficiency of the industrialization process and, thus, to improve the standard
of living of the Hungarian people.

NOTES

1. The data are based on György Karádi, "Hungary's Fourth Five-Year Plan, 1971-1975," Marketing
in Hungary, No. 3 (1970), pp. 2-11.

2. The information in this section is based
chiefly on the various articles in Otto Gadó, ed.,
Közgazdasági Szabályozó Rendszerünk Továbbfejlesztése
(The Continued Development of Our Economic Regulatory
System) (Budapest: Közgazdasági és Jogi Könyvkiadó,
1970).

3. Decision No. 19 (1970) of the Presidium of
the Hungarian People's Republic.

4. Figyelö, February 10, 1971, p. 1.

5. For an interesting discussion of industrial
enterprise investment plans over the 1971-75 period,
see Zoltán Bösze and Gábor Havas, "A Vállalatok
Fejlesztési Szándékairól" (Enterprise Investment
Plans), Gazdaság, March, 1971, pp. 50-71.

6. Figyelö, April 21, 1971, p. 1.

7. Jan Tinbergen, "Do Communist and Free Econ-
omies Show a Converging Pattern?" Soviet Studies,
No. 4 (April, 1961), pp. 333-41; Walt W. Rostow,
The Stages of Economic Growth (New York: Cambridge
University Press, 1960); and John Kenneth Galbraith,
The New Industrial State (New York: New American
Library, 1968).

8. Galbraith, The New Industrial State, pp.
396 and 398, respectively.

BIBLIOGRAPHY

BOOKS

Balassa, Béla. The Hungarian Experience in Economic Planning. New Haven: Yale University Press, 1959.

Bokor, János. A Vállalatok Nyereségérdekeltsége, A Vállalati Alapok (The Profit Interest of Enterprises, Enterprise Funds). Budapest: Közgazdasági és Jogi Könyvkiadó, 1968.

Buda, István, and Pongrácz, László. Személyi Jövedelmek, Anyagi Érdekeltség, Munka-Erö Gazdalkodás (Personal Income, Financial Interest, Labor Economics). Budapest: Közgazdasági és Jogi Könyvkiadó, 1968.

Dózsa, Lajos, ed. A Vállalati Belsö Mechanizmus Fejlesztésének Gyakorlati Kérdései (The Practical Issues of the Further Development of the Internal Enterprise Mechanism). Budapest: A Magyar Szocialista Munkáspárt Központi Bizottságának Gazdaságpolitikai Osztálya, 1971.

Facsády, Kálmán. A Vállalatok Külkereskedelmi Tevékenységének Tervezése az Uj Gazdaságirányitás Rendszerében (The Planning of Enterprise Foreign Trade Activities Under the New Economic Mechanism). Budapest: Közgazdasági és Jogi Könyvkiadó, 1969.

Farmer, Richard N., and Richman, Barry M. Comparative Management and Economic Progress. Homewood, Ill.: Richard D. Irwin, 1965.

Ficzere, Lajos. Az Állami Vállalat a Gazdaságirányitás Uj Rendszerében (The State Enterprise Under the New Economic Mechanism). Budapest: Közgazdasági és Jogi Könyvkiadó, 1970.

177

Friss, István, ed. Reform of the Economic Mechanism
     in Hungary. Budapest: Academic Publishing Co.,
     1969.

Fürész, István, and Katócs, Albert. A Termékfogal-
     mazás Uj Rendje (The New System of Distribution).
     Budapest: Közgazdasági és Jogi Könyvkiadó, 1967.

Gadó, Otto, ed. Közgazdasági Szabályozó Rendszerünk
     Továbbfejlesztése (The Continued Development of
     Our Economic Regulatory System). Budapest:
     Közgazdasági és Jogi Könyvkiadó, 1970.

Galbraith, John Kenneth. The New Industrial State.
     New York: New American Library, 1968.

Grossman, Gregory, ed. Value and Plan, Economic Cal-
     culation and Organization in Eastern Europe.
     Berkeley: University of California Press, 1960.

Helmreich, Ernst C. Hungary. New York: Frederick
     A. Praeger, 1957.

Kornai, János. Overcentralization in Economic Admin-
     istration, A Critical Analysis Based on Experi-
     ence in Hungarian Light Industry. New York:
     Oxford University Press, 1959.

Likert, Rensis. The Human Organization: Its Manage-
     ment and Value. New York: McGraw-Hill, 1967.

Magyar Statisztikai Zsebkönyv 1970 (Hungarian Statis-
     tical Pocketbook 1970). Budapest: Központi
     Statisztikai Hivatal, 1971.

Marx, Karl. Capital. Chicago: Charles H. Kerr and
     Co., 1907.

Nyers, Rezsö. 25 Kérdés és Válasz Gazdaság-Politikai
     Kérdésekröl (25 Questions and Answers Concern-
     ing Economic Policy Questions). Budapest:
     Kossuth Könyvkiadó, 1969.

Róka, Róbert. Bankhitel a Gyakorlatban (Bank Credit
     in Practice). Budapest: Közgazdasági és Jogi
     Könyvkiadó, 1970.

Rostow, Walt W. The Stages of Economic Growth.
    New York: Cambridge University Press, 1960.

Spulber, Nicholas. The Economics of Communist East-
    ern Europe. Cambridge, Mass.: The M.I.T. Press,
    1957.

_____. Socialist Management and Planning. Bloom-
    ington: Indiana University Press, 1971.

Statisztikai Évkönyv 1969 (Statistical Yearbook 1969).
    Budapest: Központi Statisztikai Hivatal, 1970.

Szabó, Kálmán, ed. A Vállalati Belsö Mechanizmus
    Helyzete és Fejlödésének Föbb Vonásai (Condi-
    tions of the Internal Enterprise Mechanism and
    Its Major Developmental Features). Budapest:
    A Magyar Szocialista Munkáspárt Központi Bizot-
    tságának Gazdaságpolitikai Osztálya, 1969.

Wilcsek, Jenö. Vállalati Tervezés a Gazdaságirányitás
    Uj Rendszerében (Enterprise Planning Under the
    New Economic Mechanism). Budapest: Közgazdasági
    és Jogi Könyvkiadó, 1967.

                         ARTICLES

Balassa, Béla. "The Economic Reform in Hungary."
    Economica, XXXIII (February, 1970).

Berend, Iván T. "The Historical Background of the
    Recent Economic Reforms in East Europe (The
    Hungarian Experience)." East European Quarterly,
    No. 3 (September, 1963).

Bösze, Zoltán, and Havas, Gábor. "A Vállalatok Fej-
    lesztési Szándékairól" (Enterprise Investment
    Plans). Gazdaság (Economics), March, 1971.

Csikós-Nagy, Béla. "The New Hungarian Price System."
    Reform of the Economic Mechanism in Hungary.
    Edited by István Friss. Budapest: Academic
    Publishing Co., 1969.

Fall, Levente. "A Gazdasági Verseny és Marketing" (Economic Competition and Marketing). Marketing-Piackutatás (Marketing-Market Research), No. 4 (1968).

Faluvégi, Lajos. "A Szabályozási Rendszer és a Preferenciák" (The Regulatory System and Preferential Treatment). Gazdaság (Economics), March, 1971.

Ferge, Zsuzsa, and Rupp, Kálman. "A Munkaerö és Életszínvonal Távlati Tervezési Hipotéziseinek Vitája" (The Discussion Concerning the Long-Range Hypotheses on Labor Conditions and the Standard of Living). Gazdaság (Economics), December, 1970.

Jánossy, Ferenc. "The Origins of Contradictions in Our Economy and the Path to Their Solution." Eastern European Economics, Summer, 1970.

Karádi, György. "Hungary's Fourth Five-Year Plan, 1971-1975." Marketing in Hungary, No. 3 (1970).

Kardos, György. "A Gazdasági Reform és Könyvkiadás" (The Economic Reform and Book Publishing). Kortárs (The Contemporary), (1969).

Lange, Oscar. "Marxian Economics and Modern Economic Theory." Marxism. Edited by Michael Curtis. New York: Atherton Press, 1970.

Lauter, Géza Peter. "The Changing Role of Marketing in the Eastern European Socialist Economies." Journal of Marketing, No. 4 (October, 1971).

_____. "Sociological, Cultural and Legal Factors Impeding Decentralization of Authority in Developing Countries." Academy of Management Journal, No. 3 (September, 1969).

Megyeri, Endre. "Marketing Tapasztalatok a Hazai Ipari, Bel és Külkereskedelmi Vállalatoknál" (The Marketing Experiences of Domestic and Foreign-Trade Industrial and Commercial Enter-

prises). Marketing-Piackutatás (Marketing-
Market Research), No. 1 (1970).

Nagy, Tamás. "The Hungarian Economic Reform, Past
and Future." Papers and Proceedings of the
Eighty-Third Meeting (American Economic Association, May, 1971).

Nyers, Rezsö. "Utunk, Céljaink, Elveink--Egy Neg-
yedszázad Tükrében" (Our Road, Objectives and
Principles in the Mirror of a Quarter Century).
Gazdaság (Economics), April, 1970.

Rédei, Jenö. "Marketing a Szocialista Gazdaságban".
(Marketing in the Socialist Economy). Figyelö
(Observer), January 1, 1969.

Szabó, László. "A Piackutatás Aktuális Problémái"
(Current Problems of Market Research). Market-
ing-Piackutatás (Marketing-Market Research),
No. 1 (1971).

_____. "Vállalati Üzletpolitika--Szocialista
Marketing" (Enterprise Policies--Socialist Marketing). Figyelö (Observer), January 1, 1969.

Tannenbaum, Arnold; Mozina, Stane; Jerovsek, Janez;
and Likert, Rensis. "Testing a Management
Style." European Business, No. 27 (Autumn,
1970).

Tinbergen, Jan. "Do Communist and Free Economies
Show a Converging Pattern?" Soviet Studies,
No. 4 (April, 1961).

Tüü, Lászlóné. "Az Ipari Termelés Ütemessége, 1968-
70" (Industrial Production Patterns, 1968-70).
Gazdaság (Economics), March, 1970.

Varga, György. "Távlati Tervezés a Magyar Vállalatoknál" (Long-Range Planning in Hungarian Enterprises). Közgazdasági Szemle (Economic Review),
May, 1970.

Wilcsek, Jenö. "Marketing a Szocialista Gazdaságban"
    (Marketing in the Socialist Economy). Figyelö
    (Observer), December 11, 1968.

_____. "Piackutatás és Szabályozott Piac" (Market
    Research and the Regulated Market). Marketing-
    Piackutatás (Marketing-Market Research), No. 4
    (1968).

_____. "The Place and Functions of the State-
    Owned Enterprises in the New System of Economic
    Control and Management." Reform of the Economic
    Mechanism in Hungary. Edited by István Friss.
    Budapest: Academic Publishing Co., 1969.

                PERIODICALS AND NEWSPAPERS

Belpolitikai Szemle (Review of Domestic Politics),
    June 18, 1958.

Figyelö (Observer), January 21, February 25, March
    11, March 18, April 8, April 22, December 16,
    December 23, 1970; January 13, January 20,
    February 10, February 24, March 17, March 31,
    April 21, April 28, May 23, May 26, June 2,
    July 14, 1971.

Magyar Közlöny (Hungarian Gazette), October 17, 1961;
    October 8, 1967.

Magyar Nemzet (Hungarian Nation), July 17, 1962.

Marketing-Piackutatás (Marketing-Market Research),
    No. 1 (1970).

Népakarat (People's Will), November 12, 1957.

Népszabadság (People's Freedom), September 7, 1960;
    June 14, November 26, 1961; June 6, October 10,
    1962; June 16, July 13, 1963; November 21, 1965;
    April 10, 1966; January 9, January 26, February
    22, September 22, 1968; February 2, 1969.

Népszava (People's Word), January 4, 1961.

Pártélet (Party Life), October, 1967.

Társadalmi Szemle (Social Review), No. 3 (1951).

INDEX

Fock, Jenő, 39
Foreign trade, 56-58, 123-30, 167-69; agreements in, 168; and balance-of-payments position, 67; and branch multiplier, 154; and import limitations, 57, 167; licenses for, 56, 155; nature of, 124; and price-differential reserve funds, 157-58; price multiplier in, 57, 124; and subsidies, 107, 153; and transfer ruble, 128
France, 36, 130

Galbraith, John Kenneth, 171
German Democratic Republic, 27, 168
Gerő, Ernő, 5

Hungarian Working People's Party: Central Committee of, 8, 33-34, 39, 100; Economic Policy Committee of, 34; relationship to management of, 36, 39, 100; role of, 5, 8; Second Congress of, 6; Tenth Congress of, 100

Incentive system, 53-56, 120-23, 162-67
Income: differentiation of, 82, 121-22; of industrial workers, 84; of managers, 81; of population, 76
Industrial authority structure, 8-9, 24, 42, 99
Interest rate: level of, 110; role of, 25
International Labor Organization, 61
Investment: activities related to, 110-15, 161; and bidding procedures, 159-60; composition of, 111; and cost overruns, 113; efficiency of, 110-11, 159; grants for, 160; priorities in, 161; types of, 50

Karl Marx University of Economic Science, 61

Labor: discipline of, 27, 115, 118, 119; fringe benefits for, 70; mobility of, 85-86, 117; morale of, 83, 134; productivity of, 27, 66, 69, 115, 117, 119, 162; quality of, 116, 118; training of, 97-98, 115-16, 119
Labor Code, 44, 51-52, 85, 115
Labor union: and collective bargaining, 52, 85; role of, 52, 85, 100-1; veto right of, 52-53, 85, 100
"Le Plan," 36
Living standard, 71

Management: attitudes of, 134-35, 166, 170; and bargaining, 18, 96; development of, 60-62, 138; practices of, 18; risk-taking of, 20-21, 135; sanctions for, 55; selection standards for, 12-13, 61, 79; social status of, 81, 86
Market place: characteristics of, 91, 94; limits of, 38; role of, 36-38, 95
Market research, 92
Marketing: performance of, 91, 135-36; teaching of, 61
Marx, Karl, 135
Marxism-Leninism, 34, 62, 90-91
Material-supply system: improvements in, 155-56; limitations of, 44-45, 101-5; negative effects of, 19-20 (see also National Materials and Price Office)
Ministry: branch, 43, 99-100; of Domestic Trade, 43; of Finance, 12, 43, 149, 157, 160; of Foreign Trade, 5, 35, 56, 58, 60; functional, 42-43, 99-100; of Heavy Industry, 43; of Labor, 43, 85, 116; of Light Industry, 43; of Metallurgy and Engineering, 43
Motivation: of managers, 15, 54-55, 120-21, 166; of supporting personnel, 16, 54-55, 120-21; types of, 16-17; of workers, 16, 54-55, 120-21

ABOUT THE AUTHOR

GEZA PETER LAUTER, Associate Professor in the School of Government and Business Administration, The George Washington University, has been a student of international management problems for some time.

Currently director of the international business program at GWU, he studied and worked in Hungary for many years. He has also lived and worked in England, Canada, and Turkey, where he spent three years with Cornell University under a Cornell-Agency for International Development contract.

His articles on various international management problems have appeared in various leading journals in the field. Dr. Lauter received a B.A. in German and English from the Institute of Foreign Languages in Budapest, Hungary, in 1954. His further studies include a B.A. in Economics and a Ph.D. in Management from the University of California at Los Angeles.